Unbreakable
Honor

Standing Firm in
a Changing World

Tom Sotis

Unbreakable Honor

ISNB # 978-1-300-94663-2

Imprint: Lulu.com

To my good friend

Andrew Smith

who exemplifies honor and integrity.

Acknowledgments

The journey of writing *Unbreakable Honor* has been as much an exploration of universal ideals as it has been a study of their relativity. Words like honor, fairness, justice, honesty, integrity, ethics, and respect hold immense power, but their meanings shift across cultures, contexts, and individuals. What may be considered honorable in one society could be seen differently in another; what is deemed just in one moment may be questioned in the next.

This book seeks to illuminate the nuanced nature of these concepts while celebrating their enduring significance. Each reader brings their own life experiences, beliefs, and cultural perspectives to these terms, breathing into them personal meaning. It is this diversity of interpretation that makes these ideals both challenging and profound.

I wish to express my gratitude to those who inspired this exploration—the mentors, friends, and thinkers who challenged my assumptions and expanded my understanding. To my readers: thank you for your willingness to engage with these ideas, for grappling with their complexities, and for reflecting on how they resonate in your own life.

Unbreakable Honor is, above all, a conversation—a testament to the human spirit's quest for meaning and the strength it takes to embody these ideals, even in their most relative forms. May we each strive to live with courage in pursuit of what these values mean to us and to the world we wish to build.

Thank you for joining me on this journey

Contents

Introduction: Rediscovering Honor in a Complex World

Honor is a concept as old as humanity itself, deeply embedded in the fabric of societies across the globe. It has been the subject of countless stories, philosophies, and cultural traditions, shaping our understanding of what it means to live a good and principled life. Yet, in today's fast-paced and often cynical world, the notion of honor can sometimes feel antiquated or out of touch with modern realities. This book seeks to redefine and reinvigorate our understanding of honor, exploring its foundational elements, challenges, and relevance in our personal, professional, and public lives.

Defining Honor: A Foundational Concept

At its core, honor is about living in alignment with one's values and principles. It encompasses integrity, respect, accountability, and a commitment to doing what is right, even when no one is watching. Honor is more than a set of rules or a rigid code of conduct; it is a deeply personal and evolving commitment that guides our actions and decisions. This foundational concept of honor serves as the starting point of our exploration, laying the groundwork for understanding its multifaceted nature and how it influences every aspect of our lives.

The Pillars of Honor: Integrity and Truthfulness

Integral to the concept of honor are the pillars of integrity and truthfulness. Integrity involves a steadfast adherence to moral and ethical principles, consistently aligning actions with values regardless of the circumstances. It requires a willingness to be honest with oneself and others, fostering trust and credibility. Truthfulness goes hand in hand with integrity, encompassing not only honesty in words but also the courage to stand by the truth, even when it is inconvenient or uncomfortable. These pillars of honor are not just abstract ideals; they are practical, everyday commitments that shape how we interact with the world around us.

In a time when misinformation and deceit often seem to dominate public discourse, the importance of truthfulness and integrity cannot be overstated. They serve as beacons that guide us through ethical dilemmas and complex situations, providing a clear path forward when faced with difficult choices. By embracing these pillars, we lay the foundation for a life of honor that is not swayed by the shifting tides of convenience or expedience.

Honor as Moral Obligation

Honor also carries with it a profound sense of moral obligation. It is the internal compass that drives us to do what is right, even when it is not the easiest or most beneficial path. This moral imperative is what compels individuals to act with courage, integrity, and selflessness, often in the face of adversity. Whether it's standing up against injustice, speaking out against wrongdoing, or simply making choices that reflect our values, the moral obligation of honor is a powerful force that transcends personal gain and connects us to a higher purpose.

This sense of obligation is not just about adhering to societal norms or expectations; it is about holding oneself to a higher standard, driven by an intrinsic desire to contribute to the greater good. Honor as moral obligation challenges us to rise above self-interest and consider the broader impact of our actions, encouraging us to be leaders, advocates, and agents of positive change in our communities and beyond.

Honor and Justice: Standing Up for What's Fair

Central to the concept of honor is the pursuit of justice. Honor calls us to stand up for what is fair and just, to advocate for those who are marginalized, and to challenge systems of inequality and oppression. It involves a commitment to fairness in our dealings with others, a dedication to upholding the rights and dignity of all individuals, and a readiness to confront injustice whenever and wherever it arises.

Standing up for justice is not always easy, and it often requires significant personal sacrifice. It demands moral courage—the backbone of honor—to speak out, take action, and resist the pressure to remain silent or complicit. This book delves into the relationship between honor and justice, exploring how individuals and communities can embody these values in their everyday lives. By examining historical and contemporary examples of honorable acts in the pursuit of justice, we gain a deeper understanding of the transformative power of standing up for what is right.

The Backbone of Honor: Courage and Resilience

Courage is the backbone of honor. Without courage, the commitment to live honorably would crumble under the weight of fear, temptation, or external pressures. Courage enables individuals to uphold their values and convictions, even when faced with significant challenges. It is the force that allows us to overcome fear, confront adversity, and act with integrity in all circumstances.

Resilience, closely related to courage, is the ability to persevere in the face of setbacks and to continue striving for honorable behavior despite difficulties. Living with honor is not about being perfect; it is about the willingness to learn from mistakes, recover from failures, and keep moving forward with a renewed commitment to one's principles. This book explores how courage and resilience can be cultivated and how they play a vital role in the journey of living with honor.

Honor in Personal Relationships

Honor is not limited to grand public acts or professional conduct; it is equally important in our personal relationships. In friendships, family dynamics, and romantic partnerships, honor fosters trust, loyalty, and respect. It guides us to treat others with kindness, to keep our promises, and to act with honesty and integrity in all our interactions.

This book examines how honor can strengthen personal relationships, providing practical insights into how to navigate conflicts, communicate effectively, and build deeper connections through honorable behavior. By prioritizing honor in our relationships, we create a foundation of mutual respect and understanding that enriches our lives and the lives of those we care about.

Honor in Professional and Public Life

In the professional and public spheres, honor plays a critical role in shaping leadership, decision-making, and ethical conduct. Whether in business, politics, or community service, honor serves as a compass that guides individuals to act with integrity, prioritize the common good, and build trust with those they serve. Dishonorable behavior in these settings can have far-reaching consequences, eroding public trust and undermining the credibility of institutions.

This book explores how honor influences professional and public life, offering guidance on how to uphold ethical standards, make principled decisions, and inspire others to act with integrity. By embracing honor in these arenas, we contribute to a more just, transparent, and accountable society.

Honor Across Cultures: A Global Perspective

Honor is a universal value, but its expression varies across cultures. From the collectivist traditions of East Asia to the individualistic values of the West, the concept of honor is shaped by diverse cultural, historical, and social contexts. Understanding these variations provides a richer, more nuanced perspective on what it means to live honorably.

This book takes a global view of honor, examining how different cultures perceive and practice it. By exploring common threads and unique variations, we gain insights into the ways in which cultural values shape our understanding of honorable behavior. This global perspective encourages us to embrace a more inclusive and empathetic approach to honor, recognizing the diversity of human experience and the shared principles that unite us.

Challenges to Honor: Temptations and Tests

The path of honor is not without its challenges. Temptations such as greed, fear, and peer pressure constantly test our resolve, while external pressures can push us toward compromise or complacency. This book addresses these challenges head-on, offering strategies for staying true to one's values in the face of adversity. It emphasizes the importance of resilience, self-awareness, and a strong support network in navigating the complexities of living with honor.

Living with Honor: Daily Practice and Personal Growth

Ultimately, living with honor is a daily practice and a lifelong journey of personal growth. It involves integrating ethical principles into every aspect of life, from small daily decisions to significant life choices. This book provides practical guidance on how to cultivate honor as a habit, how to inspire honorable actions in others, and how to leave a lasting legacy through principled living.

Living with honor is not just about the actions we take; it is about the legacy we leave behind. By embracing the values of integrity, courage, and respect, we can make a positive impact on the world and inspire others to do the same. This book is an invitation to embark on the journey of living with honor, to strive for personal and collective growth, and to contribute to a more just, compassionate, and honorable world.

Chapter 1: Defining Honor: A Foundational Concept

Understanding the Origins and Evolution of the Concept of Honor

Honor is a complex and multifaceted concept that has been a central value in human societies for centuries. Its origins are deeply rooted in the social and cultural fabric of ancient civilizations, where honor served as a guiding principle for behavior, social interactions, and community cohesion. To understand honor fully, we must trace its evolution through different historical epochs, explore its various manifestations, and examine how it has adapted to changing societal norms and expectations.

Origins of Honor: Ancient Civilizations and Early Concepts

The concept of honor can be traced back to ancient civilizations such as Greece, Rome, China, and Japan, where it was closely linked to social status, duty, and personal conduct. In ancient Greece, honor (known as "timē") was a core value that determined a person's worth and reputation within society. It was often associated with achievements in battle, wisdom, and service to the state. Greek heroes like Achilles and Hector were revered not only for their prowess in combat but also for their unwavering commitment to honor, which drove their actions and decisions.

Similarly, in ancient Rome, honor (or "honor" in Latin) was a fundamental aspect of the Roman ethos. It was deeply connected to the concept of "virtus," which encompassed courage, strength, and moral integrity. Roman citizens, particularly those in positions of power, were expected to uphold their honor through acts of bravery, loyalty, and public service. Honor was seen as both a personal attribute and a public obligation, with significant social and political consequences for those who failed to live up to its standards.

In ancient China, the concept of honor was closely tied to Confucian principles of "li" (ritual propriety) and "ren" (benevolence). Confucius emphasized the importance of personal integrity, respect for elders, and fulfilling one's societal roles with honor and dignity. The Chinese notion of honor extended beyond individual actions to encompass familial and communal responsibilities, reflecting a broader understanding of honor as a collective value that shaped social harmony.

In Japan, the samurai code of "bushido" epitomized the ideals of honor, loyalty, and discipline. Bushido, which translates to "the way of the warrior," dictated the conduct of samurai warriors, who were expected to live and die with honor. The practice of "seppuku" (ritual suicide) was considered an honorable way to atone for failure or dishonor, underscoring the profound weight placed on maintaining one's honor in Japanese culture.

Evolution of Honor: Medieval to Modern Times

As societies evolved, so too did the concept of honor, adapting to new social structures, political systems, and cultural influences. During the medieval period in Europe, honor became closely associated with chivalry and knighthood. Knights were bound by a code of conduct that emphasized bravery, courtesy, and the protection of the weak. Honor was not only a personal attribute but also a social currency that determined one's standing within the feudal hierarchy.

In the Renaissance and Enlightenment eras, the concept of honor began to shift from a purely martial and aristocratic ideal to a broader notion of personal integrity and moral virtue. Thinkers like John Locke and Immanuel Kant explored the ethical dimensions of honor, linking it to concepts of individual rights, dignity, and the pursuit of personal excellence. This intellectual shift reflected a growing emphasis on the internal, self-regulatory aspects of honor, as opposed to purely external displays of status or power.

In the modern era, the concept of honor has continued to evolve, influenced by changing societal norms, legal frameworks, and global cultural exchanges. While traditional notions of honor as a matter of personal and familial reputation still persist in many cultures, contemporary understandings of honor often emphasize individual autonomy, ethical integrity, and social responsibility. Honor is now seen as a universal value that transcends cultural boundaries, encompassing a commitment to honesty, respect for others, and adherence to one's principles.

Differentiating Honor from Related Concepts: Respect, Dignity, and Reputation

While honor shares similarities with concepts like respect, dignity, and reputation, it is important to distinguish these terms to fully grasp the unique nature of honor.

Honor vs. Respect

Respect is a recognition of the value or worth of someone or something. It can be earned through actions, achievements, or qualities that inspire admiration. Respect is often given to individuals who demonstrate competence, kindness, or authority. Unlike honor, which is deeply personal and tied to one's moral code, respect is more outward-facing and situational. For example, a person might respect a colleague for their professional skills without necessarily feeling that the colleague embodies honor.

Honor, on the other hand, is an intrinsic quality that reflects a person's commitment to their values and principles. It is self-regulated and does not solely depend on external validation. While respect can be lost or gained based on specific actions, honor is maintained through consistent adherence to one's moral code, regardless of external recognition.

Honor vs. Dignity

Dignity refers to the inherent worth of every human being, deserving of respect and ethical treatment. It is a universal concept that underpins human rights and ethical behavior. Dignity is not contingent on one's actions or status; it is an intrinsic value that all individuals possess simply by virtue of being human.

Honor, while also tied to personal worth, is more closely linked to an individual's actions and choices. It involves a conscious effort to uphold certain standards of behavior and ethical conduct. While dignity is an inherent right, honor is something that must be cultivated and maintained through one's actions.

Honor vs. Reputation

Reputation is the perception others have of an individual based on their past behavior, actions, and character. It is a social construct that can be influenced by public opinion, gossip, or the judgments of others. Reputation can be positive or negative and is often subject to change based on new information or actions.

Honor, however, is less about public perception and more about an individual's internal moral compass. While reputation is shaped by how others see us, honor is defined by how we see ourselves and the standards we hold ourselves to. A person can maintain their honor even if their reputation is damaged, as long as they remain true to their principles.

The Significance of Honor in Personal, Cultural, and Historical Contexts

Honor plays a significant role in shaping individual behavior, societal norms, and historical narratives. It serves as a guiding principle that influences how people interact with others, make decisions, and perceive their place in the world.

Personal Significance

On a personal level, honor is a source of self-respect and inner strength. It provides a framework for making ethical decisions, setting boundaries, and navigating life's challenges. When individuals act with honor, they align their actions with their values, fostering a sense of integrity and authenticity. This alignment can lead to greater self-confidence, resilience, and fulfillment.

Honor also acts as a moral compass, guiding individuals through complex ethical dilemmas. In situations where the right course of action is unclear, a commitment to honor can provide clarity and direction. For example, choosing to speak the truth, even when it is difficult, reflects a dedication to honor that transcends personal convenience or fear of consequences.

Cultural Significance

Culturally, honor has been a defining element of social identity and community cohesion. In many societies, honor is tied to family, tradition, and collective values. It serves as a benchmark for acceptable behavior and helps to establish social order. For example, in many Middle Eastern, Asian, and Mediterranean cultures, honor is closely linked to family reputation and social standing. Acts that bring honor or shame to the family can have profound social implications, affecting relationships, marriage prospects, and community acceptance.

Honor also plays a critical role in shaping cultural narratives and ideals. Stories of heroic figures, both historical and fictional, often emphasize themes of honor, sacrifice, and moral courage. These narratives reinforce cultural values and serve as models for honorable behavior, inspiring individuals to uphold similar ideals in their own lives.

Historical Significance

Throughout history, honor has been a driving force behind significant events, conflicts, and social movements. It has motivated individuals and groups to take action, whether in defense of their principles, their communities, or their nations. Honor has been cited as a justification for duels, wars, and revolutions, as well as acts of resistance, reform, and social justice.

For example, the concept of honor played a central role in the chivalric codes of medieval knights, the samurai ethos in Japan, and the warrior traditions of various Indigenous cultures. In each of these contexts, honor was not only a personal attribute but also a societal expectation that governed behavior and relationships.

In more recent history, the civil rights movements of the 20th century can be seen as a collective struggle for honor, dignity, and justice. Activists who stood up against racial discrimination, gender inequality, and social injustice did so out of a sense of moral obligation and honor, challenging societal norms and advocating for the inherent worth and dignity of all individuals.

How Honor Influences Our Decisions and Interactions with Others

Honor is more than just a personal virtue; it is a guiding principle that shapes our interactions with others and informs our decisions. It influences how we conduct ourselves in various aspects of life, from personal relationships to professional endeavors, and it plays a crucial role in building trust, credibility, and respect.

Honor in Personal Relationships

In personal relationships, honor fosters trust, loyalty, and mutual respect. When individuals act honorably, they prioritize honesty, keep their promises, and treat others with consideration and kindness. This creates a foundation of trust that strengthens relationships and allows them to flourish.

Honor also involves standing by others in times of need and acting with integrity, even when it is difficult. For example, supporting a friend who is going through a challenging time, standing up against bullying or injustice, or admitting when one is wrong are all acts of honor that enhance personal relationships.

Moreover, honor can guide individuals in setting healthy boundaries and making decisions that align with their values.

It encourages self-respect and the courage to walk away from relationships that are harmful or do not honor one's worth.

Honor in Professional and Public Life

In professional settings, honor is closely linked to ethical conduct, accountability, and respect for others. Acting with honor in the workplace involves being truthful, reliable, and fair in dealings with colleagues, clients, and stakeholders. It means taking responsibility for one's actions, adhering to ethical standards, and striving to contribute positively to the work environment.

Honor in public life extends to leadership and governance, where it is essential for building public trust and credibility. Leaders who act with honor are transparent, accountable, and committed to serving the public good. They make decisions based on principles rather than personal gain, and they are willing to stand by their convictions, even when it is unpopular or challenging.

Honor as a Social Contract

On a broader scale, honor functions as a social contract that underpins societal norms and expectations. It sets standards for behavior that promote fairness, respect, and cooperation within communities. When individuals act honorably, they contribute to a culture of trust and mutual respect, which in turn strengthens social bonds and fosters a sense of belonging.

In many ways, honor acts as a deterrent to unethical or harmful behavior. The desire to maintain one's honor and avoid shame can motivate individuals to act in accordance with societal values and expectations. For example, the fear of bringing dishonor to oneself or one's family can discourage actions that are considered socially unacceptable, such as dishonesty, theft, or betrayal.

Honor as a Source of Personal Fulfillment

Ultimately, honor is a source of personal fulfillment and self-actualization. Living with honor allows individuals to align their actions with their values, leading to a sense of authenticity and inner peace. It fosters a positive self-image and contributes to overall well-being, as individuals who act honorably are more likely to experience pride in their actions and satisfaction in their relationships.

Honor also provides a sense of purpose and direction, guiding individuals toward goals and pursuits that are meaningful and aligned with their principles. It encourages a life of integrity, courage, and ethical responsibility, offering a path to personal growth and fulfillment.

Conclusion

Honor is a foundational concept that transcends time, culture, and personal circumstances. It is a guiding principle that shapes our behavior, decisions, and interactions with others, influencing every aspect of our lives. By understanding the origins and evolution of honor, differentiating it from related concepts, and recognizing its significance in personal, cultural, and historical contexts, we can better appreciate its value and strive to live honorably in our own lives.

Honor is not just a reflection of how others see us; it is a testament to how we see ourselves and the standards we hold ourselves to. It is a commitment to doing what is right, standing up for what is fair, and having the courage to live according to our values. In a world that is often marked by uncertainty and complexity, honor remains a steadfast guide, offering a clear and compelling path to a life of purpose, integrity, and fulfillment.

Chapter 2: The Pillars of Honor: Integrity and Truthfulness

Honor is deeply rooted in the values of integrity and truthfulness, serving as a foundation for how individuals conduct themselves in both personal and professional spheres. Integrity and truthfulness are not just traits that enhance one's reputation; they are essential components of a life guided by honor. This chapter delves into the intricate relationship between honor, integrity, and honesty, highlighting the significance of being truthful and trustworthy in all aspects of life. Additionally, it explores how integrity shapes personal and professional reputations and provides real-world examples of integrity in action.

Exploring the Relationship Between Honor, Integrity, and Honesty

Honor, integrity, and honesty are closely interconnected, each reinforcing the other in a symbiotic relationship that forms the basis of ethical behavior. To understand this relationship, it is essential to define these concepts and examine how they overlap and support one another.

Defining Integrity

Integrity refers to the quality of being honest and having strong moral principles. It involves consistently adhering to ethical standards, even when it is inconvenient, difficult, or goes against one's immediate self-interest. Integrity is about being true to oneself and acting in alignment with one's values, regardless of external pressures or temptations.

Integrity encompasses various aspects, including:

- **Consistency:** Acting in accordance with one's values and principles across different situations.

- **Honesty:** Being truthful in one's words, actions, and intentions.

- **Accountability:** Taking responsibility for one's actions and decisions, especially when mistakes are made.

- **Moral Courage:** Standing up for what is right, even in the face of adversity or opposition.

Defining Honesty

Honesty is the quality of being truthful, sincere, and free from deceit. It involves presenting facts as they are, without manipulation or distortion, and being transparent in one's communications. Honesty is a fundamental aspect of integrity, as it reflects a commitment to truth and a rejection of falsehood.

Honesty is manifested in various ways, including:

- **Truthfulness:** Accurately conveying information and avoiding lies or half-truths.

- **Transparency:** Being open and clear about one's intentions, actions, and decisions.

- **Sincerity:** Expressing genuine thoughts, feelings, and intentions without pretense or deceit.

- **Reliability:** Being dependable and following through on promises and commitments.

How Integrity and Honesty Relate to Honor

Honor is the overarching concept that encompasses both integrity and honesty. It is the commitment to living a life guided by ethical principles, moral courage, and a dedication to doing what is right. Honor involves not only acting in accordance with one's values but also upholding the values of society, community, or profession.

The relationship between honor, integrity, and honesty can be summarized as follows:

- **Honor as the Guiding Principle:** Honor provides the overarching framework for ethical behavior, encompassing the values of integrity and honesty.

- **Integrity as the Core Value:** Integrity is the consistent adherence to ethical principles and moral standards, forming the foundation of honorable behavior.

- **Honesty as the Expression of Integrity:** Honesty is the practical manifestation of integrity, demonstrated through truthful communication and transparent actions.

Together, these three concepts create a cohesive approach to ethical living. A person of honor acts with integrity and honesty, consistently upholding their values and principles in all aspects of life.

The Importance of Being Truthful and Trustworthy in All Aspects of Life

Truthfulness and trustworthiness are essential qualities that underpin meaningful relationships, personal credibility, and societal cohesion. Being truthful and trustworthy is not just about avoiding dishonesty; it is about building a foundation of trust, respect, and integrity that enhances every aspect of life.

Building Trust and Credibility

Trust is the cornerstone of all relationships, whether personal, professional, or societal. Trustworthiness is earned through consistent honesty, reliability, and transparency. When individuals are truthful and trustworthy, others feel confident in relying on them, whether it be in friendships, business dealings, or community interactions.

Credibility, which is closely linked to trustworthiness, is the quality of being believable and reliable. A person who is known for their honesty and integrity gains credibility, making it easier for others to have faith in their words and actions. Credibility is especially important in leadership, where trust in one's character and judgment is essential for effective decision-making and influence.

Fostering Respect and Mutual Understanding

Truthfulness fosters respect and mutual understanding in relationships. When people are honest with one another, they create an environment of openness and authenticity. This allows for genuine connections, where individuals feel valued and heard. In contrast, dishonesty can lead to misunderstandings, conflicts, and a breakdown of communication.

Respect is a two-way street; being truthful demonstrates respect for others, while receiving honesty from others fosters reciprocal respect. In both personal and professional settings, mutual respect is crucial for collaboration, conflict resolution, and long-term success.

Enhancing Personal Integrity and Self-Respect

Living truthfully and with integrity enhances one's sense of self-respect and personal fulfillment. When individuals act in alignment with their values and principles, they experience a sense of coherence and authenticity. This internal alignment fosters self-confidence and a positive self-image.

On the other hand, dishonesty and lack of integrity can lead to internal conflict, guilt, and a diminished sense of self-worth. Consistently compromising one's values erodes self-respect and can lead to a cycle of negative behaviors that further distance individuals from their true selves.

Promoting Ethical Behavior in Society

Honesty and integrity are essential for the functioning of ethical societies. They promote transparency, accountability, and fairness, which are critical for justice and social cohesion. When individuals, institutions, and leaders act with integrity, they set a positive example for others and contribute to a culture of trust and ethical behavior.

In contrast, dishonesty and lack of integrity can undermine social structures, leading to corruption, exploitation, and a loss of public trust. For society to thrive, individuals must uphold the values of truthfulness and integrity in their interactions and decision-making processes.

How Integrity Shapes Personal and Professional Reputations

Integrity plays a pivotal role in shaping both personal and professional reputations. A reputation built on integrity is one of the most valuable assets an individual can possess, as it reflects a consistent commitment to ethical behavior, honesty, and trustworthiness.

Personal Reputation

A person's reputation is a reflection of their character, values, and actions. Integrity is the foundation of a strong personal reputation, as it demonstrates a commitment to doing what is right, even when it is difficult or inconvenient. Individuals who act with integrity are seen as dependable, honorable, and worthy of respect.

In personal relationships, integrity fosters trust and reliability. Friends, family members, and partners are more likely to rely on and confide in someone who consistently demonstrates honesty and integrity. A reputation for integrity also attracts like-minded individuals, leading to positive and supportive relationships.

Integrity also shapes how individuals perceive themselves. Living with integrity allows people to take pride in their actions and decisions, leading to greater self-confidence and self-respect. Conversely, compromising one's integrity can lead to feelings of guilt, shame, and self-doubt.

Professional Reputation

In the professional realm, integrity is a critical determinant of success and credibility. A professional reputation built on integrity enhances one's career prospects, as it reflects a commitment to ethical standards, accountability, and reliability. Employers, colleagues, and clients value individuals who demonstrate integrity, as it signals that they can be trusted to act in the best interests of the organization or stakeholders.

Integrity in the workplace manifests in various ways, including:

- **Honest Communication:** Being transparent and truthful in all communications, whether with colleagues, clients, or supervisors.

- **Accountability:** Taking responsibility for one's actions, admitting mistakes, and making amends when necessary.

- **Consistency:** Upholding ethical standards consistently, regardless of the situation or potential consequences.

- **Fairness:** Treating others with respect and fairness, without favoritism or bias.

A reputation for integrity is especially important for leaders, as it sets the tone for organizational culture and influences the behavior of others. Leaders who act with integrity inspire trust, loyalty, and commitment from their teams. They create a work environment where ethical behavior is valued and encouraged, leading to greater collaboration, productivity, and success.

The Long-Term Impact of Integrity on Reputation

While reputation can be built or damaged by individual actions, integrity is a long-term investment that pays dividends over time. A consistent track record of integrity builds a solid reputation that withstands challenges and setbacks. Even in difficult situations, individuals with a reputation for integrity are more likely to be given the benefit of the doubt, as others trust that their actions are guided by ethical principles.

On the other hand, a lack of integrity can have lasting negative consequences for one's reputation. Dishonesty, deceit, and unethical behavior can lead to a loss of trust, damaged relationships, and limited opportunities. Rebuilding a damaged reputation is often a long and challenging process, underscoring the importance of consistently acting with integrity.

Real-World Examples of Integrity in Action

Integrity is not just an abstract concept; it is a practical value that is demonstrated through everyday actions and decisions. Real-world examples of integrity in action highlight the importance of staying true to one's values, even in challenging or high-stakes situations.

Whistleblowing: Speaking Truth to Power

Whistleblowers are individuals who expose unethical, illegal, or harmful practices within organizations, often at great personal risk. Whistleblowing is a powerful example of integrity in action, as it involves prioritizing the public good over personal gain or safety. Whistleblowers demonstrate moral courage by standing up against wrongdoing, even when it means facing retaliation, job loss, or legal consequences.

One notable example is Dr. Jeffrey Wigand, a former tobacco executive who blew the whistle on the tobacco industry's knowledge of the harmful effects of smoking and their efforts to manipulate nicotine levels in cigarettes. Despite facing intense pressure, threats, and legal battles, Wigand chose to expose the truth, ultimately contributing to greater public awareness and regulatory changes in the tobacco industry.

Business Integrity: Putting Ethics Above Profits

Businesses that prioritize integrity over profits set a powerful example for ethical leadership and corporate responsibility. One such example is Patagonia, an outdoor clothing company known for its commitment to environmental sustainability and ethical business practices. Patagonia has consistently demonstrated integrity by prioritizing transparency, fair labor practices, and environmental stewardship, even when it means making decisions that may not maximize short-term profits.

For instance, Patagonia's "Don't Buy This Jacket" campaign urged consumers to consider the environmental impact of their purchases and encouraged them to buy only what they need. This campaign, while counterintuitive from a traditional marketing perspective, reflected the company's commitment to reducing waste and promoting responsible consumption.

Integrity in Leadership: Standing Firm on Principles

Leaders who act with integrity set a positive example for others and inspire trust and confidence. One such leader is Nelson Mandela, whose commitment to justice, equality, and reconciliation guided his actions throughout his life. Despite spending 27 years in prison for his opposition to apartheid in South Africa, Mandela emerged with a commitment to peace and unity rather than revenge. His integrity and moral courage helped lead South Africa through a peaceful transition to democracy and earned him global respect and admiration.

Mandela's leadership demonstrated that integrity is not just about personal conduct but also about making decisions that align with one's values, even in the face of immense challenges. His commitment to forgiveness, inclusivity, and human rights set a powerful example of integrity in action.

Everyday Integrity: Small Acts of Honesty

Integrity is not limited to grand gestures or high-profile actions; it is also reflected in everyday choices and interactions. Simple acts of honesty, such as returning a lost wallet, admitting a mistake, or refusing to cut corners, demonstrate integrity in action. These small, everyday decisions contribute to a culture of trust and ethical behavior, reinforcing the importance of living with integrity in all aspects of life.

For example, consider a student who finds an answer key to an upcoming exam. While the temptation to use the key may be strong, choosing to do the right thing by not cheating reflects integrity. This decision not only upholds the student's honor but also reinforces their commitment to personal growth and learning.

Similarly, a business owner who chooses to pay their employees fairly, even during difficult financial times, demonstrates integrity by prioritizing ethical conduct over personal gain. These everyday examples show that integrity is not about perfection but about consistently striving to do what is right.

Conclusion

Integrity and truthfulness are the pillars of honor, shaping personal and professional reputations and guiding ethical behavior in all aspects of life. By exploring the relationship between honor, integrity, and honesty, we gain a deeper understanding of how these values intersect to create a cohesive framework for ethical living. Being truthful and trustworthy is not just a matter of avoiding dishonesty; it is a commitment to living authentically, building trust, and fostering respect.

Integrity shapes our reputations, influences our decisions, and defines how we interact with others. It is the foundation of personal fulfillment, professional success, and societal cohesion. Through real-world examples of integrity in action, we see the transformative power of living with honor, demonstrating that integrity is not just an ideal but a practical and essential aspect of a meaningful and honorable life. As we strive to uphold integrity and truthfulness in our own lives, we contribute to a world where honor, trust, and ethical behavior are valued and celebrated.

Chapter 3: Honor as Moral Obligation

Honor is often perceived as a reflection of one's personal values, integrity, and ethical conduct. At its core, honor is not just about reputation or social recognition; it is deeply tied to the concept of moral obligation. This chapter delves into the intricate relationship between honor and moral obligation, exploring how the ethical imperative to do what is right—regardless of the difficulties or consequences—drives honorable behavior. By understanding how moral obligation shapes our decisions and actions, we can better navigate ethical dilemmas with honor as our guiding principle.

Understanding the Concept of Moral Obligation

Moral obligation refers to the ethical duty or responsibility to act in accordance with one's moral beliefs and principles. It involves a commitment to doing what is right, just, and fair, even when such actions may not be convenient, popular, or personally advantageous. Moral obligations are deeply rooted in our understanding of what is ethically correct, and they often require individuals to go beyond self-interest to consider the broader impact of their actions on others and society as a whole.

Defining Moral Obligation

Moral obligation can be defined as the duty to act according to ethical principles and moral values. This duty arises from a sense of right and wrong that is informed by personal beliefs, cultural norms, religious teachings, or philosophical reasoning. Unlike legal obligations, which are enforced by laws and regulations, moral obligations are self-imposed and guided by an individual's conscience.

Moral obligations are often framed by questions such as:

- What is the right thing to do in this situation?

- How will my actions affect others?

- Am I upholding my values and principles through my actions?

- Am I acting with integrity and respect for others?

The concept of moral obligation extends beyond individual actions to include collective responsibilities, such as caring for the environment, advocating for social justice, and contributing to the well-being of the community. Moral obligations are not limited to personal interactions but also encompass broader societal and global considerations.

The Sources of Moral Obligation

Moral obligations can arise from various sources, including:

- **Personal Values:** Individual beliefs about what is right and wrong, often shaped by upbringing, experiences, and introspection.

- **Cultural Norms:** Shared values and expectations within a society or community that influence perceptions of ethical behavior.

- **Religious Teachings:** Moral guidelines provided by religious doctrines, scriptures, and spiritual leaders that emphasize the importance of ethical conduct.

- **Philosophical Principles:** Ethical theories and philosophical reasoning, such as deontology, utilitarianism, or virtue ethics, that provide a framework for understanding moral duties.

Regardless of their source, moral obligations serve as a compass that guides individuals in making ethical decisions and taking actions that align with their values.

Moral Obligation and Personal Responsibility

A key aspect of moral obligation is personal responsibility. Individuals are accountable for their actions and decisions, and they bear the moral consequences of those choices. This sense of responsibility is intrinsic to the concept of honor, as it reflects a commitment to upholding one's ethical standards and living in accordance with one's principles.

Moral obligation requires individuals to take ownership of their actions, even when those actions may have challenging or uncomfortable consequences. It involves a willingness to confront difficult truths, admit mistakes, and make amends when necessary. By embracing personal responsibility, individuals demonstrate honor and integrity, reinforcing their commitment to doing what is right.

The Ethical Imperative to Do What Is Right, Even in the Face of Challenges

The ethical imperative to do what is right, regardless of the challenges or obstacles, is a defining characteristic of honorable behavior. Acting in accordance with moral obligations often requires courage, perseverance, and a willingness to face adversity. It is in these moments of ethical challenge that the true measure of honor is revealed.

The Courage to Act Honorably

Honor is closely linked to courage—the courage to stand up for what is right, to speak the truth, and to take ethical actions even when it is difficult or risky. Moral obligations often call for acts of bravery, such as defending the vulnerable, opposing injustice, or making ethical decisions that may be unpopular or disadvantageous.

Courageous individuals who act honorably do so because they recognize the importance of their moral obligations. They understand that ethical conduct is not contingent on convenience or personal gain but is a reflection of their commitment to their values. This courage is evident in individuals who challenge corruption, resist unethical practices, or advocate for social change, despite the potential for personal repercussions.

Overcoming Temptations and Challenges

Fulfilling moral obligations requires individuals to overcome temptations, pressures, and challenges that may lead them away from ethical behavior. Temptations such as greed, fear, peer pressure, and the desire for approval can undermine one's commitment to doing what is right. Honor involves resisting these temptations and staying true to one's moral convictions.

For example, a business leader may face the temptation to cut corners or engage in unethical practices to maximize profits. However, an honorable leader recognizes their moral obligation to act with integrity, prioritize the well-being of their employees, and uphold ethical standards. By resisting short-term temptations and making decisions that align with their values, they demonstrate honor and reinforce their commitment to ethical leadership.

The Role of Perseverance in Upholding Moral Obligations

Perseverance is essential in upholding moral obligations, especially when faced with prolonged or intense challenges. Honor requires individuals to remain steadfast in their commitment to doing what is right, even when progress is slow or opposition is strong. Perseverance involves continuing to act ethically, even in the face of setbacks, criticism, or adversity.

Historical figures such as Mahatma Gandhi, Martin Luther King Jr., and Malala Yousafzai exemplify the perseverance required to uphold moral obligations. Each of these individuals faced significant challenges, including imprisonment, violence, and threats to their lives, yet they remained committed to their principles of nonviolence, justice, and equality. Their perseverance in the pursuit of honor not only shaped their personal legacies but also inspired transformative social change.

The Importance of Consistency in Ethical Behavior

Consistency is a key element of honor and moral obligation. Honorable individuals consistently uphold their values and ethical standards across different situations and contexts. They do not waver in their commitment to doing what is right, even when faced with conflicting interests or external pressures.

Consistency in ethical behavior builds trust and credibility, as others recognize that the individual's actions are guided by a stable and reliable moral compass. This consistency is particularly important in leadership, where the actions of those in positions of authority set the tone for organizational culture and influence the behavior of others.

How Moral Obligation Drives Honorable Behavior

Moral obligation serves as the driving force behind honorable behavior, compelling individuals to act in ways that reflect their ethical values and principles. By understanding the motivations and mechanisms that underlie moral obligation, we can gain insight into how it shapes honorable actions and decisions.

Moral Obligation as a Guiding Force

Moral obligation acts as a guiding force that directs individuals toward ethical behavior. It serves as an internal compass that helps individuals navigate complex situations and make decisions that align with their values. When faced with ethical dilemmas, individuals who are guided by moral obligation are more likely to choose actions that reflect honor and integrity.

For example, consider a journalist who uncovers evidence of corruption within a powerful institution. Despite the potential risks to their career or personal safety, the journalist feels a moral obligation to report the truth and hold those in power accountable. This sense of duty to the public and commitment to ethical journalism drives the journalist to act honorably, even in the face of significant challenges.

The Role of Conscience in Moral Obligation

Conscience plays a central role in moral obligation, acting as the internal voice that alerts individuals to the ethical dimensions of their actions. Conscience provides the emotional and cognitive cues that guide individuals toward honorable behavior, such as feelings of guilt when acting against one's values or a sense of fulfillment when upholding one's principles.

Individuals who act with honor are attuned to their conscience and are willing to listen to its guidance, even when it points them toward difficult or uncomfortable actions. By prioritizing the voice of conscience over external pressures or temptations, they reinforce their commitment to moral obligation and honor.

The Influence of Empathy and Compassion

Empathy and compassion are important drivers of moral obligation, as they allow individuals to connect with the experiences and needs of others. When individuals feel empathy for those who are suffering or vulnerable, they are more likely to recognize their moral obligation to act in ways that alleviate harm or promote well-being.

Honorable behavior often involves acts of kindness, support, and advocacy on behalf of others. For example, a bystander who witnesses bullying may feel a moral obligation to intervene and support the victim, driven by empathy and a desire to uphold principles of fairness and justice. This sense of connection to others reinforces the individual's commitment to acting honorably.

The Impact of Moral Exemplars

Moral exemplars—individuals who consistently demonstrate honorable behavior—serve as powerful influences on others' sense of moral obligation. By observing the actions of moral exemplars, individuals gain insight into how to navigate ethical challenges and are inspired to emulate similar behavior.

Moral exemplars can be found in various contexts, including family members, teachers, community leaders, historical figures, and fictional characters. Their actions provide concrete examples of how to live honorably, and their stories reinforce the importance of moral obligation as a guiding principle.

For instance, the story of Rosa Parks refusing to give up her seat on a segregated bus serves as a powerful example of moral courage and the ethical imperative to challenge injustice. Parks's actions, driven by her moral obligation to stand up for her rights and the rights of others, inspired a broader civil rights movement and highlighted the transformative impact of acting honorably in the face of systemic discrimination.

Navigating Ethical Dilemmas with Honor as a Guide

Ethical dilemmas—situations in which individuals must choose between conflicting moral principles or values—are a common aspect of life. Navigating these dilemmas with honor as a guide requires careful reflection, a commitment to ethical principles, and a willingness to make difficult choices.

Identifying Ethical Dilemmas

Ethical dilemmas often arise when individuals are faced with competing values, such as honesty versus loyalty, individual rights versus the greater good, or personal gain versus social responsibility. Recognizing the ethical dimensions of a situation is the first step in navigating dilemmas with honor.

To identify ethical dilemmas, individuals can ask themselves questions such as:

- What are the key values or principles at stake in this situation?

- Are there conflicting moral obligations that need to be considered?

- How will my actions affect others, both directly and indirectly?

- What are the potential consequences of each available option?

By reflecting on these questions, individuals can gain a clearer understanding of the ethical challenges they face and the factors that must be weighed in their decision-making process.

Applying Ethical Principles

When navigating ethical dilemmas, applying ethical principles can provide a framework for making honorable decisions. Ethical principles such as honesty, fairness, respect, and responsibility serve as benchmarks for evaluating potential actions and determining the most honorable course.

For example, consider a manager who discovers that a valued employee has been falsifying reports to meet performance targets. The manager faces an ethical dilemma between protecting the employee's job and upholding the integrity of the organization. By applying ethical principles such as honesty and accountability, the manager can navigate the dilemma with honor, making a decision that aligns with the organization's values and sets a positive example for others.

Seeking Guidance and Perspective

Navigating ethical dilemmas with honor often involves seeking guidance from others who can provide perspective and support. Consulting with trusted mentors, colleagues, or advisors can help individuals explore different viewpoints, identify potential blind spots, and consider the broader implications of their actions.

Additionally, reflecting on the actions of moral exemplars or drawing on ethical frameworks such as virtue ethics, deontology, or consequentialism can provide valuable insights into how to approach ethical challenges with honor.

Making Decisions with Integrity

Ultimately, navigating ethical dilemmas with honor requires making decisions that align with one's values and moral obligations. This involves acting with integrity, even when the choices are difficult or the outcomes are uncertain. Honorable individuals prioritize ethical considerations over personal gain or convenience, demonstrating a commitment to doing what is right.

For example, a whistleblower who exposes unethical practices within their organization may face significant personal and professional risks. However, by choosing to act in accordance with their moral obligation to uphold honesty and protect the public interest, they demonstrate honor and integrity, reinforcing the importance of ethical conduct.

Reflecting on the Outcomes

After navigating an ethical dilemma, reflecting on the outcomes and lessons learned can reinforce the importance of honor and moral obligation in decision-making. Reflection allows individuals to assess the impact of their actions, consider how they might approach similar situations in the future, and refine their understanding of their own values and principles.

Reflection also provides an opportunity to acknowledge the complexities of ethical decision-making and the potential for growth and learning. By embracing the ongoing journey of ethical reflection and self-improvement, individuals can continue to navigate dilemmas with honor and reinforce their commitment to moral obligation.

Conclusion

Honor as moral obligation is a powerful guiding principle that shapes ethical behavior, drives honorable actions, and provides a framework for navigating complex dilemmas. By understanding the concept of moral obligation and recognizing its connection to honor, individuals can cultivate a deeper commitment to doing what is right, even in the face of challenges.

Moral obligation is not just an abstract ideal; it is a practical and essential aspect of living honorably. It requires courage, perseverance, empathy, and a willingness to take personal responsibility for one's actions. By embracing moral obligation as a guiding force, individuals can act with integrity, build trust, and contribute to a more ethical and just society.

As we strive to live honorably and uphold our moral obligations, we are reminded that honor is not merely a reflection of how others perceive us; it is a testament to our dedication to our values and principles. It is a commitment to ethical living that transcends personal interests and challenges us to be our best selves in service to others and the greater good.

Chapter 4: Honor and Justice: Standing Up for What's Fair

Honor and justice are deeply intertwined values that guide individuals in their pursuit of fairness, equality, and moral integrity. While honor reflects a personal commitment to ethical conduct, justice represents the broader societal ideal of treating individuals with fairness and impartiality. Together, they form a powerful force that drives individuals to stand up for what is right and challenge injustices in their communities and beyond. This chapter explores the critical role of justice in the concept of honor, the importance of advocating for fairness and equality, practical ways to stand up for others, and real-world examples of honorable acts in the pursuit of justice.

Defining Justice and Its Critical Role in the Concept of Honor

Justice is a foundational principle that underpins the functioning of ethical societies. It represents the pursuit of fairness, equality, and moral rightness in human interactions and institutions. Justice is not merely about adhering to laws; it encompasses a deeper commitment to treating individuals with respect, protecting their rights, and ensuring that everyone has an equal opportunity to thrive. In the context of honor, justice serves as a guiding force that compels individuals to act with integrity, challenge inequality, and advocate for the well-being of others.

Defining Justice

Justice can be defined as the principle of fairness and moral rightness that governs human behavior and societal interactions. It involves treating individuals with

47

impartiality, upholding their rights, and ensuring that everyone receives what they are due. Justice encompasses various dimensions, including:

- **Distributive Justice:** The fair distribution of resources, opportunities, and benefits within a society.

- **Procedural Justice:** The fairness and transparency of processes and decision-making, ensuring that individuals are treated equitably.

- **Retributive Justice:** The fair and proportional punishment of wrongdoing, with the aim of maintaining order and deterring future harm.

- **Restorative Justice:** The emphasis on repairing harm, reconciling relationships, and addressing the needs of victims and offenders.

Justice is not a static concept; it evolves over time as societies develop new understandings of fairness, rights, and equality. It is a dynamic and multifaceted value that reflects humanity's ongoing quest for a more just and equitable world.

The Role of Justice in the Concept of Honor

Honor is intrinsically linked to the pursuit of justice. An honorable individual is committed to upholding the principles of fairness and treating others with respect and dignity. Justice provides the ethical framework that informs honorable behavior, guiding individuals to act in ways that promote the well-being of others and address inequities.

The relationship between honor and justice can be understood through the following dimensions:

- **Moral Responsibility:** Honor involves a moral responsibility to do what is right, even when it is difficult. This responsibility extends to advocating for justice and standing up against injustices that harm individuals or communities.

- **Integrity and Consistency:** An honorable individual consistently upholds the values of justice in their actions and decisions. This consistency reinforces their commitment to fairness and strengthens their credibility as a person of honor.

- **Empathy and Advocacy:** Honor requires individuals to empathize with others and advocate for their rights and well-being. Justice, as a core aspect of honor, compels individuals to challenge discrimination, inequality, and injustice wherever they occur.

By embracing justice as a critical component of honor, individuals are inspired to take meaningful actions that promote fairness and contribute to the creation of a just society.

The Importance of Advocating for Fairness and Equality

Advocating for fairness and equality is not only a matter of personal integrity; it is essential for the advancement of a just and harmonious society. Fairness ensures that individuals are treated equitably and that their rights are respected, while equality seeks to eliminate barriers and disparities that prevent individuals from achieving their full potential. Together, these principles form the foundation of a society where individuals can coexist peacefully and thrive.

The Ethical Imperative of Fairness

Fairness is a fundamental aspect of justice that involves treating individuals with impartiality and ensuring that they are not subjected to bias or discrimination. It is an ethical imperative that requires individuals to consider the needs and perspectives of others, make decisions that are just and equitable, and avoid actions that cause harm or disadvantage.

Fairness is not only about treating people the same; it also involves recognizing and addressing the unique challenges and circumstances that individuals may face. This nuanced understanding of fairness allows for the implementation of measures that promote equity, ensuring that everyone has access to the resources and opportunities they need to succeed.

The Pursuit of Equality

Equality is the principle that all individuals, regardless of their background, characteristics, or circumstances, deserve equal rights, opportunities, and treatment. The pursuit of equality involves challenging systemic barriers and social inequalities that perpetuate discrimination and injustice. This includes addressing issues such as:

- **Racial and Ethnic Discrimination:** Combatting prejudice and ensuring that individuals of all races and ethnicities are treated with respect and have equal access to opportunities.

- **Gender Equality:** Promoting the rights and empowerment of women and individuals of all genders, and challenging gender-based discrimination and violence.

- **Economic Inequality:** Addressing disparities in wealth, income, and access to resources, and advocating for policies that promote economic justice.

- **Disability Rights:** Ensuring that individuals with disabilities have equal access to education, employment, and public services, and are treated with dignity and respect.

Advocating for equality is a collective effort that requires the participation of individuals, communities, and institutions. It involves both challenging existing injustices and working proactively to create inclusive and equitable environments.

The Role of Advocacy in Promoting Justice

Advocacy is the act of speaking up, taking action, and using one's voice to support the rights and needs of others. It is a powerful tool for promoting justice and driving social change. Advocacy can take many forms, including:

- **Raising Awareness:** Educating others about issues of injustice and inequality, and highlighting the experiences of marginalized or oppressed communities.

- **Policy Advocacy:** Working to influence laws, policies, and practices that affect the rights and well-being of individuals and communities.

- **Community Engagement:** Mobilizing individuals and groups to take collective action in support of justice and equality.

- **Allyship:** Standing in solidarity with those who are directly affected by injustice, and using one's privilege or platform to amplify their voices.

Advocacy is a demonstration of honor in action, as it reflects a commitment to standing up for what is right and working to create a fairer and more just world.

How to Stand Up for Others and Fight Against Injustice

Standing up for others and fighting against injustice is an honorable act that requires courage, empathy, and a commitment to ethical principles. Whether in everyday interactions or larger societal contexts, individuals have the power to make a difference by challenging injustice and supporting those in need.

Recognizing Injustice

The first step in standing up against injustice is recognizing when it occurs. Injustice can manifest in various forms, including discrimination, harassment, exploitation, and systemic inequality. It is important to be vigilant and attentive to the experiences of others, especially those from marginalized or vulnerable communities.

Recognizing injustice also involves questioning norms, policies, and practices that may perpetuate harm or disadvantage. This critical awareness enables individuals to identify areas where intervention or advocacy is needed.

Speaking Out

One of the most direct ways to stand up against injustice is to speak out against it. Speaking out involves expressing opposition to unfair or harmful actions, whether through direct communication, public statements, or social media platforms. It is an act of moral courage that challenges the status quo and calls attention to the need for change.

Speaking out can take many forms, including:

- **Confronting Discriminatory Behavior:** Addressing bias, prejudice, or harmful actions when they occur, whether in personal interactions, workplaces, or public spaces.

- **Supporting Those Affected by Injustice:** Offering words of support, validation, and encouragement to individuals who are experiencing injustice, and amplifying their voices.

- **Using One's Platform for Advocacy:** Leveraging one's position, influence, or social media presence to raise awareness about issues of injustice and advocate for change.

Speaking out is a demonstration of honor, as it reflects a commitment to standing up for fairness and challenging actions that undermine the rights and dignity of others.

Taking Action

In addition to speaking out, taking concrete actions to address injustice is a vital aspect of honorable behavior. Actions can range from individual efforts to organized collective movements, and they can include:

- **Volunteering:** Contributing time, skills, or resources to organizations that work to support marginalized communities or address social justice issues.

- **Advocating for Policy Change:** Engaging in efforts to influence policies and laws that affect the rights and well-being of individuals and communities. This can include lobbying, petitioning, or participating in grassroots campaigns.

- **Providing Direct Support:** Offering assistance to individuals or groups affected by injustice, whether through financial support, mentorship, or providing resources and opportunities.

Taking action demonstrates a proactive commitment to justice and reflects the principle that honor is not just about intentions but also about tangible efforts to create positive change.

Building Allyship and Solidarity

Allyship and solidarity involve standing in support of those who are directly affected by injustice and using one's privilege or influence to advocate for their rights. Being an ally means actively listening, learning, and taking responsibility for challenging one's own biases and behaviors that may contribute to inequality.

Solidarity goes beyond individual actions; it involves building collective strength and working together to address systemic issues. This can include forming coalitions, participating in protests or demonstrations, and supporting the leadership of marginalized communities in the fight for justice.

Allyship and solidarity are expressions of honor, as they demonstrate a commitment to collective action and the belief that everyone has a role to play in creating a just society.

Examples of Honorable Acts in the Pursuit of Justice

Throughout history and in contemporary society, countless individuals have demonstrated honor by standing up for justice and fighting against injustice. These honorable acts serve as powerful examples of how commitment to fairness, equality, and moral integrity can drive meaningful change.

The Civil Rights Movement

The American Civil Rights Movement of the 1950s and 1960s is a powerful example of collective action in the pursuit of justice. Activists such as Martin Luther King Jr., Rosa Parks, and John Lewis, along with countless others, demonstrated honor by challenging racial segregation and advocating for the rights of African Americans.

The movement employed nonviolent resistance, civil disobedience, and legal challenges to confront systemic racism and achieve significant gains in civil rights. Acts such as the Montgomery Bus Boycott, the March on Washington, and the Selma to Montgomery marches highlighted the importance of standing up for justice, even in the face of violence and opposition.

The Civil Rights Movement exemplifies how honor and justice can drive transformative social change and inspire future generations to continue the fight for equality.

Malala Yousafzai: Advocating for Girls' Education

Malala Yousafzai, a Pakistani activist for girls' education, is a contemporary example of honor in action. At the age of 15, Malala survived an assassination attempt by the Taliban, who targeted her for advocating for the education of girls in her region. Despite the danger, Malala continued to speak out for the rights of girls to receive an education, emphasizing the importance of equality and justice.

In 2014, Malala became the youngest-ever recipient of the Nobel Peace Prize, recognizing her courageous advocacy for education and gender equality. Her commitment to standing up for what is right, even in the face of life-threatening challenges, reflects the essence of honor and justice.

Nelson Mandela: Fighting Apartheid in South Africa

Nelson Mandela, a South African anti-apartheid revolutionary and political leader, dedicated his life to fighting racial segregation and promoting justice in his country. Mandela spent 27 years in prison for his opposition to apartheid, yet he remained committed to his vision of a democratic and inclusive South Africa.

Upon his release, Mandela continued to advocate for reconciliation, peace, and justice, ultimately becoming the first Black president of South Africa in 1994. Mandela's leadership and unwavering commitment to fairness and equality earned him global recognition as a symbol of honor and justice.

Everyday Acts of Honor in the Pursuit of Justice

Honor and justice are not confined to historical figures or high-profile activists; they are values that can be demonstrated in everyday actions. Acts such as speaking up against bullying, supporting marginalized individuals, advocating for inclusive policies in the workplace, or volunteering with organizations that address social issues all reflect a commitment to justice.

Honorable individuals recognize that they have the power to make a difference, whether through small gestures or larger efforts. By standing up for fairness and equality, they contribute to a culture of justice that benefits everyone.

Conclusion

Honor and justice are interconnected values that drive individuals to stand up for what is fair, challenge injustices, and advocate for the rights and well-being of others. Justice provides the ethical framework that informs honorable behavior, compelling individuals to act with integrity, empathy, and moral courage.

Advocating for fairness and equality is not only an expression of honor; it is essential for the advancement of a just and harmonious society. By recognizing injustice, speaking out, taking action, and building solidarity, individuals can make meaningful contributions to the pursuit of justice.

The examples of honorable acts in the pursuit of justice, whether through historical movements, contemporary activism, or everyday actions, serve as powerful reminders of the impact that individuals can have when they act with honor and a commitment to fairness. As we strive to live honorably and uphold the values of justice, we play a vital role in creating a more equitable and inclusive world for all.

Chapter 5: Courage: The Backbone of Honor

Courage is the foundation upon which honor is built. It is the driving force that allows individuals to uphold their values, stand by their convictions, and act with integrity, even in the face of fear, adversity, and significant personal risk. Without courage, honor becomes a fragile concept, easily compromised when challenges arise. This chapter explores the crucial role of courage in maintaining honor, how courage empowers individuals to live by their principles, the process of overcoming fear to act honorably, and real-life stories of courageous individuals who have exemplified honor.

Understanding the Role of Courage in Maintaining Honor

Courage is often defined as the ability to confront fear, pain, danger, uncertainty, or intimidation. It is not the absence of fear, but the determination to act in accordance with one's values despite that fear. In the context of honor, courage is the essential quality that allows individuals to remain steadfast in their ethical commitments, even when faced with challenges that threaten to compromise those commitments.

Courage as a Pillar of Honor

Honor demands consistency in upholding one's values and principles, regardless of the circumstances. This unwavering commitment to doing what is right, even when it is difficult, is made possible by courage. Courage serves as a pillar of honor, providing the inner strength needed to make ethical choices in the face of fear, social pressure, or personal loss.

For example, a whistleblower who exposes corporate malfeasance demonstrates courage by risking their job, reputation, and personal safety to act in alignment with their moral convictions. Without courage, the fear of retaliation or ostracism might prevent them from taking action, compromising their honor and allowing unethical behavior to continue unchecked.

Moral Courage vs. Physical Courage

While physical courage involves confronting physical threats or dangers, moral courage is the fortitude to stand up for one's beliefs, principles, and ethical standards, even when doing so is socially or personally risky. Moral courage is a key component of honor, as it reflects a deep commitment to integrity and justice that transcends personal safety or comfort.

Moral courage can manifest in various ways, such as:

- **Standing up against injustice:** Challenging discriminatory practices, unfair treatment, or unethical behavior, even when it is easier to remain silent or conform.

- **Admitting mistakes:** Taking responsibility for one's errors and making amends, rather than deflecting blame or denying wrongdoing.

- **Defending others:** Supporting and advocating for individuals who are vulnerable, marginalized, or mistreated, even when it is unpopular or inconvenient.

Moral courage is often more challenging than physical courage because it requires individuals to confront internal fears, such as the fear of rejection, failure, or loss of social standing. However, it is precisely this type of courage that is most closely aligned with the concept of honor.

Courage as a Choice

Courage is not an innate trait possessed only by a select few; it is a choice that individuals make in response to challenging situations. Choosing to act courageously means prioritizing one's values over fear, comfort, or self-interest. This choice is at the heart of honorable behavior, as it reflects a deliberate commitment to integrity and ethical conduct.

Courageous individuals recognize that honor is not a passive quality; it requires active engagement and intentional decision-making. By choosing courage, they affirm their dedication to living honorably and inspire others to do the same.

How Courage Enables Individuals to Uphold Their Values and Convictions

Courage plays a vital role in enabling individuals to uphold their values and convictions, even when doing so is fraught with difficulty. It is the force that empowers people to remain true to themselves, their beliefs, and their ethical principles, regardless of the external pressures they may face.

Standing Firm in the Face of Opposition

Upholding one's values often means standing firm in the face of opposition, whether from peers, authority figures, or societal norms. Courage enables individuals to resist conforming to behaviors or beliefs that contradict their ethical standards, even when it would be easier to go along with the crowd.

For example, an employee who refuses to participate in unethical business practices, such as falsifying reports or cutting corners, demonstrates courage by prioritizing their values over the pressure to conform. This act of defiance, driven by moral courage, upholds their honor and reinforces their commitment to integrity.

Acting with Integrity When It's Inconvenient

Courage allows individuals to act with integrity, even when it is inconvenient or costly. Upholding honor often requires making difficult choices that may involve personal sacrifice, such as losing a job, facing social ostracism, or enduring financial hardship. Courage empowers individuals to accept these sacrifices in service of their principles.

A notable example is the decision of a political leader to resign from office rather than compromise their ethical standards. This act of courage, though personally and professionally challenging, reflects a deep commitment to honor and demonstrates the value of integrity over convenience or personal gain.

Advocating for Change and Justice

Courage is also a driving force behind advocacy for change and justice. Individuals who challenge unjust systems, speak out against discrimination, or fight for the rights of others do so because they are guided by their values and a sense of moral duty. Courage enables them to take action, even when the path to change is fraught with obstacles.

Activists, reformers, and social justice advocates exemplify the courage required to uphold honor in the pursuit of a better world. Their actions are often met with resistance, hostility, or even danger, yet they persist because their convictions are stronger than their fears. This unwavering commitment to justice is a hallmark of both courage and honor.

Resisting Corruption and Temptation

Maintaining honor also involves resisting corruption, temptation, and the lure of unethical shortcuts. Courage provides the inner strength to make ethical decisions in the face of temptation, whether it be the temptation to lie, cheat, or exploit others for personal gain.

For example, a business owner who refuses to engage in bribery or unethical competition, even when it would result in financial advantage, demonstrates courage by upholding their values. This decision to act with integrity, despite the potential cost, reinforces their honor and sets a positive example for others in their industry.

Overcoming Fear and Adversity to Act Honorably

Fear and adversity are natural aspects of the human experience, and they often serve as barriers to honorable behavior. However, courage is the key to overcoming these barriers and choosing actions that align with one's values. By understanding how to confront and navigate fear, individuals can cultivate the courage needed to act honorably, even in the most challenging circumstances.

Acknowledging and Understanding Fear

The first step in overcoming fear is acknowledging its presence and understanding its source. Fear is a natural response to perceived threats, whether physical, emotional, or social. It can manifest as fear of failure, rejection, judgment, loss, or harm. Recognizing fear allows individuals to confront it directly, rather than letting it dictate their actions.

Understanding fear also involves examining the beliefs and assumptions that underlie it. For example, fear of standing up to authority may stem from a belief that dissent will lead to punishment or ostracism. By questioning these beliefs and considering alternative perspectives, individuals can reduce the power that fear holds over their decisions.

Reframing Fear as an Opportunity for Growth

Courage involves reframing fear not as a barrier, but as an opportunity for growth and self-discovery. Acting in the face of fear is a powerful way to build resilience, strengthen one's values, and deepen one's commitment to honor. By viewing fear as a challenge to be met, rather than a force to be avoided, individuals can transform their approach to difficult situations.

For example, a public speaker who feels anxious about addressing a large audience can reframe their fear as an opportunity to share their message and inspire others. This shift in perspective empowers them to move forward with courage, even if the fear remains present.

Taking Small Steps Toward Courageous Action

Courage is not always about grand gestures; it often begins with small, incremental steps that build confidence and reinforce honorable behavior. Taking small actions, such as speaking up in a meeting, setting boundaries, or admitting a mistake, can serve as foundational acts of courage that pave the way for larger, more significant actions.

By practicing courage in everyday situations, individuals develop the habit of acting honorably, even when faced with fear. These small acts of courage accumulate over time, strengthening one's ability to confront larger challenges with integrity.

Seeking Support and Building Resilience

Courage is not a solitary endeavor; seeking support from others can provide the encouragement and strength needed to act honorably. Whether through mentors, friends, colleagues, or support groups, connecting with individuals who share similar values can reinforce one's commitment to courage and honor.

Building resilience—the ability to recover from setbacks and continue moving forward—is also essential for maintaining courage in the face of adversity. Resilience allows individuals to persevere through challenges, learn from failures, and remain steadfast in their pursuit of honorable behavior.

Embracing Vulnerability as a Source of Strength

Courage and vulnerability are closely linked; embracing vulnerability is often a courageous act in itself. Vulnerability involves acknowledging one's fears, uncertainties, and limitations, and being willing to take risks despite them. This openness to vulnerability is a source of strength, as it reflects a deep commitment to authenticity and integrity.

For example, a leader who admits to not having all the answers or who seeks input from their team demonstrates vulnerability and courage. This willingness to be open and transparent fosters trust, collaboration, and a culture of honor within the organization.

Stories of Courageous Individuals Who Exemplify Honor

Throughout history and in contemporary society, countless individuals have demonstrated courage in the pursuit of honor. Their stories serve as powerful examples of how courage can drive honorable behavior, inspire others, and create lasting positive impact.

Rosa Parks: The Courage to Defy Injustice

Rosa Parks, an African American civil rights activist, is best known for her courageous act of defiance in 1955 when she refused to give up her seat to a white passenger on a segregated bus in Montgomery, Alabama. Parks's refusal to comply with discriminatory laws was not a spontaneous decision; it was a deliberate act of courage rooted in her commitment to justice and equality.

Parks's actions sparked the Montgomery Bus Boycott, a pivotal event in the Civil Rights Movement that challenged racial segregation and ultimately led to significant changes in U.S. law. Despite the risks of arrest, harassment, and threats to her safety, Parks's courage to stand up against injustice exemplified honor and inspired others to join the fight for civil rights.

Nelson Mandela: The Courage to Forgive and Reconcile

Nelson Mandela, a South African anti-apartheid revolutionary, political leader, and philanthropist, spent 27 years in prison for his opposition to the apartheid regime. Despite enduring harsh conditions and personal sacrifices, Mandela remained steadfast in his commitment to justice, equality, and the liberation of his people.

Upon his release, Mandela faced the challenge of leading a deeply divided nation toward reconciliation and peace. Instead of seeking revenge against those who had oppressed him, Mandela chose the path of forgiveness and inclusivity. His courage to embrace reconciliation and promote unity over retribution demonstrated a profound sense of honor and set a powerful example for the world.

Mandela's leadership during South Africa's transition to democracy, and his dedication to healing a nation scarred by racial injustice, earned him global respect as a symbol of courage, honor, and moral integrity.

Malala Yousafzai: The Courage to Advocate for Education

Malala Yousafzai, a Pakistani activist for girls' education, became an international symbol of courage after surviving an assassination attempt by the Taliban in 2012. Malala was targeted for her outspoken advocacy for the right of girls to receive an education, a stance that challenged the oppressive norms imposed by extremist groups in her region.

Despite the life-threatening attack, Malala refused to be silenced. She continued to speak out on behalf of girls and young women, using her platform to raise awareness about the importance of education and equality. In 2014, Malala became the youngest-ever recipient of the Nobel Peace Prize, recognizing her courageous efforts to promote education and empower young people.

Malala's story is a testament to the power of courage in the face of adversity. Her unwavering commitment to her values, even in the face of violence and opposition, exemplifies honor and has inspired millions around the world to advocate for their rights.

Captain "Sully" Sullenberger: The Courage to Act Under Pressure

On January 15, 2009, Captain Chesley "Sully" Sullenberger, a commercial airline pilot, made a courageous and life-saving decision when US Airways Flight 1549 lost engine power shortly after takeoff. Faced with the immediate threat of a catastrophic crash, Captain Sullenberger chose to perform an emergency landing in the Hudson River, successfully saving the lives of all 155 passengers and crew on board.

Captain Sullenberger's quick thinking, calm demeanor, and decisive action under extreme pressure were lauded as acts of exceptional courage and professionalism. His commitment to his duty and the safety of his passengers exemplified honor and integrity in the face of crisis.

Sullenberger's actions not only demonstrated the importance of courage in moments of critical decision-making but also highlighted the value of training, preparation, and ethical responsibility in maintaining honor.

Everyday Acts of Courage and Honor

While stories of well-known individuals provide powerful examples of courage and honor, it is important to recognize that acts of courage occur in everyday life. Ordinary people demonstrate honor through small yet significant actions, such as:

- Speaking up against bullying or discrimination in schools and workplaces.

- Supporting a friend or family member through a difficult time, even when it requires personal sacrifice.

- Standing up for ethical practices in business, even when it goes against the prevailing culture.

- Admitting a mistake and taking responsibility for one's actions, rather than deflecting blame.

These everyday acts of courage, though often less visible, are no less valuable in the pursuit of honor. They reflect the principle that courage is accessible to everyone and that honorable behavior is within reach in all aspects of life.

Conclusion

Courage is the backbone of honor, providing the strength and resilience needed to uphold one's values, stand by one's convictions, and act with integrity in the face of fear and adversity. Whether through grand acts of defiance, such as challenging systemic injustice, or through small, everyday decisions that reflect ethical commitment, courage empowers individuals to live honorably and inspire others to do the same.

Understanding the role of courage in maintaining honor allows us to recognize the importance of confronting fear, embracing vulnerability, and making choices that align with our deepest values. By cultivating courage, we reinforce our commitment to honor and set a positive example for others to follow.

The stories of courageous individuals who exemplify honor serve as powerful reminders that courage is not the absence of fear but the determination to act in spite of it. As we strive to live honorably, we can draw strength from these examples, knowing that courage is a choice we can make in every moment, and that each act of courage contributes to a more just, ethical, and honorable world.

Chapter 6: Honor in Personal Relationships

Honor plays a crucial role in shaping the quality and depth of our personal relationships. It serves as the foundation for building trust, fostering mutual respect, and creating bonds that are resilient in the face of challenges. Whether in friendships, family dynamics, or romantic partnerships, honorable behavior is essential for maintaining healthy and fulfilling connections. This chapter explores the role of honor in personal relationships, how to navigate conflicts with integrity and respect, and practical ways to be a reliable and honorable partner.

The Role of Honor in Building and Maintaining Trust in Relationships

Trust is the cornerstone of all meaningful relationships. It is the confidence that we place in others, knowing that they will act with honesty, integrity, and respect. Honor plays a pivotal role in establishing and sustaining this trust, as it reflects a commitment to ethical behavior and accountability.

Building Trust Through Consistency and Integrity

Honor in relationships is demonstrated through consistent actions that align with one's values and commitments. Consistency is key to building trust because it reassures others that they can rely on you to act predictably and dependably. This predictability is not about being rigid or inflexible but rather about maintaining integrity across different situations.

Integrity—acting in accordance with one's principles, even when it is inconvenient—reinforces trust by demonstrating that your actions are guided by a moral compass. When you consistently choose to act honorably, others feel secure in the knowledge that you are reliable and trustworthy.

For example, a friend who consistently keeps promises, shows up when needed, and speaks truthfully, even in difficult conversations, builds a strong foundation of trust. This consistency signals that their actions are not driven by convenience but by a genuine commitment to the relationship and its values.

Transparency and Honesty as Pillars of Trust

Honesty and transparency are integral components of honor in relationships. Being truthful in your words and actions fosters an environment of openness where individuals feel safe to express themselves without fear of deception or betrayal. Transparency involves being clear about your intentions, communicating openly, and addressing misunderstandings or conflicts directly.

When individuals are honest with each other, even about uncomfortable topics, it strengthens trust by reinforcing the belief that the relationship is built on a foundation of truth. This honesty also encourages reciprocal openness, allowing for deeper connections and a more authentic understanding of one another.

In romantic partnerships, for instance, honesty about feelings, expectations, and boundaries is essential for building a secure and trusting bond. A partner who values honor will prioritize truthful communication, avoiding half-truths, omissions, or evasions that could undermine the relationship.

Accountability and Responsibility in Relationships

Honor in personal relationships also involves taking responsibility for one's actions and holding oneself accountable when mistakes occur. Acknowledging errors, offering sincere apologies, and making amends are all expressions of honor that contribute to the maintenance of trust.

Accountability demonstrates that you are willing to own your actions and their impact on others, rather than deflecting blame or minimizing harm. This willingness to take responsibility is crucial in maintaining trust, as it shows that you value the relationship enough to address and resolve issues honestly.

For example, in family dynamics, a parent who admits when they have been unfair or overly harsh, and takes steps to repair the relationship with their child, models honorable behavior. This accountability not only rebuilds trust but also sets a positive example for how conflicts should be navigated with integrity.

Reliability and Dependability

Being reliable and dependable are key aspects of honor in relationships. Reliability means being there when you say you will be, following through on commitments, and showing up consistently for the people who matter to you. Dependability builds trust by providing a sense of security that others can count on you in times of need.

In friendships, reliability might look like being available for a friend who is going through a difficult time, keeping confidences, or offering support without needing to be asked. In romantic partnerships, it involves being a steady presence, offering emotional and practical support, and being responsive to your partner's needs.

When individuals demonstrate reliability, they affirm their honor and reinforce the trust that underpins healthy relationships. This dependability is not about perfection; rather, it is about the consistent effort to be present, engaged, and committed to the well-being of others.

Honorable Behavior in Friendships, Family, and Romantic Partnerships

Honorable behavior is essential across all types of personal relationships, from friendships to family connections to romantic partnerships. In each context, honor serves as a guiding principle that shapes interactions, supports mutual respect, and fosters a sense of belonging and connection.

Honorable Behavior in Friendships

Friendships are built on shared experiences, mutual support, and a sense of camaraderie. Honor in friendships involves being a loyal and trustworthy friend who prioritizes the relationship and consistently acts with integrity.

Key elements of honorable behavior in friendships include:

- **Loyalty:** Standing by your friends, offering support in good times and bad, and being a reliable confidant.

- **Respect for Boundaries:** Understanding and respecting your friend's needs, preferences, and limits, and being mindful of their boundaries.

- **Constructive Honesty:** Providing honest feedback and perspectives when needed, but always with kindness and consideration for your friend's feelings.

- **Empathy and Compassion:** Being attuned to your friend's emotions and offering empathy and understanding, even when you may not fully agree with their choices.

Honorable friendships are marked by a commitment to each other's well-being, where friends feel valued, respected, and supported in their personal journeys.

Honorable Behavior in Family Relationships

Family relationships are often complex and multifaceted, encompassing a range of roles, responsibilities, and expectations. Honor in family dynamics involves respecting familial bonds, acting with integrity, and striving to create a supportive and nurturing environment.

Honorable behavior in family relationships includes:

- **Respect and Understanding:** Valuing each family member's individuality, honoring generational differences, and approaching conflicts with empathy and patience.

- **Dependability:** Being a consistent and reliable presence for your family, whether through daily interactions, support in crises, or simply being available when needed.

- **Forgiveness and Reconciliation:** Acknowledging that conflicts and misunderstandings are a natural part of family life, and approaching these challenges with a willingness to forgive and seek reconciliation.

- **Setting Healthy Boundaries:** Recognizing the importance of boundaries and maintaining a balance between familial obligations and personal well-being.

Honoring family relationships does not mean avoiding conflict or sacrificing one's own needs; rather, it involves a commitment to navigating familial dynamics with respect, care, and integrity.

Honorable Behavior in Romantic Partnerships

Romantic partnerships thrive on a foundation of trust, intimacy, and mutual respect. Honor plays a critical role in creating a secure and loving relationship where both partners feel valued and supported.

Key aspects of honorable behavior in romantic partnerships include:

- **Commitment and Fidelity:** Being faithful to your partner, honoring the promises and commitments made, and prioritizing the relationship.

- **Open Communication:** Maintaining honest and open communication, expressing needs and concerns, and actively listening to your partner's perspective.

- **Respect and Equality:** Treating your partner with respect, valuing their autonomy, and fostering a relationship that is based on equality and mutual support.

- **Conflict Resolution with Integrity:** Approaching conflicts with a focus on resolution, rather than winning or assigning blame. Honorable partners prioritize understanding and finding common ground.

Honor in romantic partnerships is about creating a space where both individuals can grow, thrive, and be their authentic selves, knowing that their partner is committed to upholding the values of trust, respect, and integrity.

Navigating Conflicts and Challenges with Honor and Respect

Conflicts and challenges are inevitable in any relationship, but how they are handled can significantly impact the health and longevity of the connection. Navigating conflicts with honor and respect involves approaching disagreements with a focus on resolution, empathy, and maintaining the integrity of the relationship.

Approaching Conflicts with a Solutions-Oriented Mindset

Honor in conflict resolution is demonstrated through a commitment to finding solutions rather than assigning blame or winning arguments. A solutions-oriented mindset prioritizes the well-being of the relationship over individual ego, and it involves seeking common ground, compromise, and collaborative problem-solving.

Key strategies for approaching conflicts with honor include:

- **Active Listening:** Paying attention to the other person's perspective without interrupting or dismissing their feelings. Active listening shows respect and a willingness to understand their point of view.

- **Open Communication:** Clearly expressing your own needs, concerns, and feelings without resorting to accusations or defensiveness. Honorable communication involves speaking honestly while also being considerate of the other person's emotions.

- **Focusing on the Issue, Not the Person:** Addressing the specific problem at hand rather than resorting to personal attacks or bringing up unrelated past grievances. This approach keeps the conversation constructive and centered on resolution.

By maintaining a focus on solutions and treating the other person with respect, conflicts can become opportunities for growth and strengthening the relationship.

Practicing Empathy and Compassion in Conflicts

Empathy and compassion are essential for navigating conflicts honorably. Empathy involves putting yourself in the other person's shoes, trying to understand their feelings and perspective, while compassion is the desire to alleviate their discomfort or distress.

When conflicts arise, practicing empathy means recognizing that the other person may be experiencing frustration, hurt, or fear, and approaching the conversation with a desire to ease those emotions rather than exacerbate them. Compassionate responses, such as offering a sincere apology or acknowledging the other person's feelings, demonstrate honor by prioritizing the relationship over being right.

Setting Boundaries and Managing Emotions

Honor in conflict resolution also involves setting healthy boundaries and managing emotions. This means recognizing when a conversation is becoming unproductive or too heated and taking a step back to cool down and gain perspective. Setting boundaries might include agreeing to take a break and revisit the discussion later or establishing guidelines for respectful communication.

Managing emotions, such as anger, frustration, or defensiveness, is crucial for maintaining honor in conflicts. It involves self-regulation, recognizing when emotions are clouding judgment, and making a conscious effort to remain calm and composed. Honorable individuals do not let their emotions dictate their actions; instead, they strive to respond thoughtfully and respectfully.

The Role of Forgiveness and Reconciliation

Forgiveness is a powerful expression of honor in relationships, as it reflects a willingness to move past hurt and work toward healing and reconciliation. Forgiveness does not mean condoning harmful behavior or forgetting past wrongs; rather, it is a conscious decision to let go of resentment and rebuild trust.

Reconciliation, the process of restoring a damaged relationship, often involves honest communication, setting new boundaries, and committing to positive changes. Honorable individuals prioritize reconciliation because they value the relationship and are willing to put in the effort required to mend it.

For example, after a significant disagreement, two friends may choose to come together, acknowledge their respective roles in the conflict, and discuss ways to prevent similar issues in the future. This process of forgiveness and reconciliation demonstrates honor by showing that both individuals are committed to preserving and strengthening their friendship.

How to Be a Reliable and Honorable Partner

Being a reliable and honorable partner is essential for maintaining healthy, fulfilling relationships. Whether in friendships, family connections, or romantic partnerships, reliability and honor are key attributes that contribute to trust, mutual respect, and lasting bonds.

Keeping Promises and Following Through

Reliability starts with keeping promises and following through on commitments. This means doing what you say you will do, showing up when expected, and being dependable in both big and small ways. When others know they can count on you, it builds a foundation of trust and reinforces your honor as a partner.

For instance, if you commit to helping a friend move, being punctual and fully present on the moving day demonstrates reliability and respect for your friend's needs. Conversely, repeatedly failing to follow through on promises can erode trust and damage the relationship.

Prioritizing Open and Honest Communication

Open and honest communication is a hallmark of an honorable partner. It involves being transparent about your feelings, needs, and boundaries, as well as listening actively and respectfully to the other person. Honorable communication is not about avoiding difficult conversations but about approaching them with sincerity and a desire to understand and resolve issues.

Honest communication also includes being upfront when you cannot meet a commitment or when your feelings have changed. By prioritizing honesty, you create a safe space where both parties can express themselves without fear of judgment or reprisal.

Showing Empathy and Support

An honorable partner is empathetic and supportive, showing genuine care for the other person's well-being. Empathy involves being attuned to the emotions and experiences of others, offering a listening ear, and responding with kindness and understanding. Support goes beyond verbal encouragement; it includes taking actionable steps to help the other person navigate challenges or achieve their goals.

For example, if your partner is going through a stressful time at work, offering to take on extra household responsibilities or providing a comforting presence can demonstrate your support and commitment to their well-being.

Respecting Boundaries and Autonomy

Respecting boundaries is a crucial aspect of honor in relationships. It involves recognizing and honoring the other person's limits, needs, and personal space, and understanding that boundaries are an expression of self-respect and self-care. Honoring boundaries is a way of showing that you value the other person's autonomy and are committed to a relationship based on mutual respect.

In romantic partnerships, respecting boundaries might include honoring your partner's need for alone time or supporting their personal interests and friendships outside of the relationship. In family dynamics, it might involve recognizing generational differences and allowing space for individual growth.

Practicing Gratitude and Appreciation

Expressing gratitude and appreciation is a simple yet powerful way to reinforce honor in relationships. Acknowledging the efforts, qualities, and contributions of the other person shows that you value and recognize their role in your life. Practicing gratitude fosters a positive atmosphere and strengthens the emotional connection between individuals.

Gratitude can be expressed through words, such as saying "thank you" or offering compliments, as well as through actions, such as thoughtful gestures or acts of kindness. By regularly expressing appreciation, you reinforce the honor and respect that underpins the relationship.

Being Willing to Learn and Grow

An honorable partner is open to learning and growing, both individually and within the context of the relationship. This means being receptive to feedback, willing to acknowledge mistakes, and committed to personal development. Growth is an ongoing process, and honorable individuals recognize that maintaining honor requires continuous self-reflection and improvement.

In relationships, this growth mindset might involve working on communication skills, addressing unhealthy patterns, or seeking counseling or guidance when needed. By prioritizing growth, you demonstrate a commitment to being the best partner you can be and to nurturing the health and vitality of the relationship.

Conclusion

Honor is a fundamental component of personal relationships, playing a critical role in building trust, fostering mutual respect, and navigating conflicts with integrity. Whether in friendships, family connections, or romantic partnerships, honorable behavior creates a foundation of reliability, empathy, and commitment that sustains and strengthens relationships over time.

By understanding the role of honor in relationships and practicing honorable behavior, individuals can cultivate connections that are resilient, supportive, and deeply fulfilling. Honor in relationships is not about perfection; it is about consistently striving to act with integrity, communicate openly, and prioritize the well-being of others.

As we navigate the complexities of personal relationships, honor serves as a guiding principle that reminds us of the importance of trust, respect, and accountability. By being reliable and honorable partners, we not only enrich our own lives but also contribute to a world where relationships are valued, respected, and cherished for the profound impact they have on our sense of belonging and connection.

Chapter 7: Honor in Professional and Public Life

Honor is a vital quality that extends beyond personal interactions and permeates professional and public life. In the workplace, business, politics, and community service, honor plays a crucial role in shaping ethical behavior, building trust, and fostering a culture of integrity. This chapter explores the significance of honor in the professional and public spheres, how it influences leadership and decision-making, the consequences of dishonorable behavior, and the importance of upholding honor in business, politics, and community service.

The Significance of Honor in the Workplace and Public Sphere

Honor in professional and public life is about more than just adhering to a set of rules or regulations; it involves a deep commitment to ethical principles, accountability, and a sense of responsibility toward others. Honor acts as a guiding force that influences how individuals conduct themselves in their professional roles and public engagements, impacting relationships, organizational culture, and societal trust.

Honor as a Foundation for Trust and Credibility

Trust and credibility are the bedrock of successful professional and public interactions. Honor underpins these qualities by ensuring that individuals act with integrity, consistency, and transparency. In the workplace, employees and leaders who demonstrate honor earn the trust of their colleagues, clients, and stakeholders, leading to stronger relationships and more effective collaboration.

In the public sphere, honor is essential for maintaining the credibility of institutions, businesses, and public figures. When leaders and organizations act honorably, they build a positive reputation that fosters public confidence and support. Conversely, a lack of honor can quickly erode trust, damage reputations, and undermine the legitimacy of institutions.

The Role of Honor in Ethical Decision-Making

Honor plays a crucial role in guiding ethical decision-making in professional and public settings. It serves as an internal compass that helps individuals navigate complex situations and make choices that align with their values and ethical standards. Honor encourages individuals to consider the broader impact of their decisions, prioritize the well-being of others, and act in ways that uphold integrity and fairness.

For example, a business leader faced with the decision to cut costs by compromising on product quality may choose to honor their commitment to customer safety and satisfaction, even if it means sacrificing short-term profits. This decision, guided by honor, reflects a dedication to ethical principles and a recognition of the long-term value of maintaining trust and credibility.

Fostering a Culture of Honor in the Workplace

Creating a culture of honor in the workplace involves promoting values such as integrity, accountability, respect, and transparency. Organizations that prioritize honor cultivate an environment where ethical behavior is expected, rewarded, and integrated into everyday practices.

Key elements of a culture of honor in the workplace include:

- **Ethical Leadership:** Leaders set the tone for organizational culture by modeling honorable behavior, making ethical decisions, and holding themselves and others accountable.

- **Clear Values and Expectations:** Organizations that clearly define their core values and ethical standards provide a framework for employees to understand what is expected of them and how to align their actions with the company's mission.

- **Open Communication:** Encouraging open communication and providing safe channels for reporting unethical behavior fosters a sense of transparency and accountability.

- **Recognition and Rewards:** Recognizing and rewarding employees who demonstrate honor and integrity reinforces the importance of these values and motivates others to follow suit.

By fostering a culture of honor, organizations can build a positive and productive work environment where employees feel valued, respected, and empowered to act ethically.

How Honor Influences Leadership, Decision-Making, and Professional Integrity

Honor is a defining characteristic of effective leadership, influencing how leaders make decisions, interact with others, and uphold professional integrity. Leaders who prioritize honor set a positive example for their teams and organizations, inspiring others to act with integrity and fostering a culture of trust and accountability.

Honor in Leadership: Setting the Standard

Leadership is not just about directing others; it is about setting a standard of behavior that reflects the values and principles of the organization. Honor in leadership involves leading by example, demonstrating consistency between words and actions, and prioritizing the needs of others over personal gain.

Honorable leaders are guided by ethical principles, such as fairness, transparency, and respect. They make decisions that align with these principles, even when faced with difficult or unpopular choices. By modeling honorable behavior, leaders create a culture of integrity that permeates the organization and encourages employees to uphold similar standards.

The Impact of Honor on Decision-Making

Decision-making is a core responsibility of leaders and professionals in all fields. Honor plays a critical role in guiding decision-making by providing a framework for evaluating options based on ethical considerations and long-term impact. Honorable decision-making involves:

- **Prioritizing Ethical Considerations:** Evaluating decisions based on their alignment with ethical principles, such as honesty, fairness, and respect for others.

- **Weighing Long-Term Impacts:** Considering the long-term consequences of decisions on stakeholders, including employees, customers, and the community, rather than focusing solely on short-term gains.

- **Transparency and Accountability:** Making decisions openly and transparently, and being willing to explain and take responsibility for the outcomes of those decisions.

For example, a public official faced with a decision about resource allocation may prioritize the needs of underserved communities, even if it is not the most politically advantageous choice. This decision, guided by honor, reflects a commitment to fairness and the well-being of all constituents.

Upholding Professional Integrity

Professional integrity is the adherence to ethical standards and principles in one's work. Honor is integral to professional integrity, as it involves consistently acting in ways that reflect honesty, accountability, and respect for others. Upholding professional integrity is essential for maintaining credibility, building trust, and fostering positive relationships with colleagues, clients, and stakeholders.

Professionals who act with honor are committed to:

- **Honesty and Transparency:** Providing truthful and accurate information, avoiding deception, and being clear about limitations or uncertainties.

- **Responsibility and Accountability:** Taking ownership of one's actions and decisions, and addressing mistakes or oversights promptly and with integrity.

- **Respect for Colleagues and Clients:** Treating others with dignity and consideration, valuing diverse perspectives, and engaging in fair and equitable practices.

Upholding professional integrity not only enhances individual reputations but also contributes to the overall ethical climate of the organization or profession.

The Impact of Dishonorable Behavior in Professional Settings

Dishonorable behavior in professional settings can have far-reaching consequences, damaging relationships, eroding trust, and undermining the integrity of organizations and institutions. Understanding the impact of dishonorable actions is essential for recognizing the importance of honor in maintaining ethical standards and positive outcomes.

Erosion of Trust and Credibility

Dishonorable behavior, such as dishonesty, unethical conduct, or abuse of power, erodes trust and credibility. When individuals or organizations act dishonorably, they undermine the confidence that others have in their intentions, actions, and decisions. This loss of trust can lead to damaged relationships, decreased morale, and a breakdown in collaboration and communication.

For example, a business that engages in deceptive marketing practices or misrepresents its products may lose the trust of its customers, leading to decreased sales, negative publicity, and long-term reputational damage. Similarly, a leader who fails to act with honor may lose the respect and loyalty of their team, resulting in decreased engagement and productivity.

Legal and Financial Consequences

Dishonorable behavior can also lead to legal and financial consequences for individuals and organizations. Unethical actions, such as fraud, corruption, or violations of regulatory standards, can result in legal penalties, fines, and costly litigation. In addition to the direct financial impact, these consequences can damage the organization's reputation, leading to a loss of business opportunities and investor confidence.

For example, major corporate scandals, such as those involving Enron or Volkswagen, demonstrate the severe financial and legal repercussions of dishonorable behavior. These cases not only resulted in significant financial losses but also highlighted the importance of upholding ethical standards to maintain the integrity of business operations.

Negative Impact on Organizational Culture

Dishonorable behavior can have a corrosive effect on organizational culture, creating an environment where unethical conduct is tolerated or even encouraged. When leaders or employees act without honor, it sets a precedent that can influence others to do the same, leading to a culture of dishonesty, misconduct, and a lack of accountability.

A toxic culture driven by dishonorable behavior can result in high employee turnover, low morale, and a lack of trust within the organization. It can also stifle innovation and creativity, as employees may feel discouraged from speaking up or sharing ideas in an environment where ethical considerations are disregarded.

Loss of Public Trust in Institutions

In the public sphere, dishonorable behavior by leaders, public officials, or institutions can lead to a loss of public trust and confidence. When public figures act without honor, it undermines the legitimacy of the institutions they represent and erodes the social contract between those in power and the communities they serve.

For example, political scandals, corruption, or abuses of power can lead to public disillusionment and a lack of faith in government or political systems. This erosion of trust can result in decreased civic engagement, voter apathy, and a diminished sense of accountability for public leaders.

Upholding honor in public life is essential for maintaining the integrity of democratic processes, fostering transparency, and ensuring that institutions serve the best interests of the people.

Upholding Honor in Business, Politics, and Community Service

Upholding honor in professional and public life is not only a personal responsibility but also a collective effort that requires commitment from individuals, organizations, and communities. By prioritizing honor in business, politics, and community service, we can create a more ethical and just society that values integrity, accountability, and respect for all.

Honor in Business: Ethical Leadership and Corporate Responsibility

In the business world, honor is reflected in ethical leadership, corporate responsibility, and a commitment to fair and transparent practices. Businesses that prioritize honor recognize that their actions have a broader impact on society, and they strive to conduct their operations in a way that aligns with ethical standards and contributes to the common good.

Key aspects of upholding honor in business include:

- **Ethical Decision-Making:** Making business decisions that prioritize the well-being of customers, employees, and the community, even when it may not maximize short-term profits.

- **Corporate Social Responsibility (CSR):** Engaging in initiatives that promote environmental sustainability, social justice, and community support, demonstrating a commitment to making a positive impact beyond financial success.

- **Transparency and Accountability:** Being open and honest about business practices, financial performance, and challenges, and taking responsibility for addressing any shortcomings or ethical concerns.

For example, companies like Patagonia and Ben & Jerry's have built their reputations on a commitment to ethical practices and social responsibility. By prioritizing honor in their business models, they have earned the trust and loyalty of customers who value their dedication to sustainability and social impact.

Honor in Politics: Integrity, Accountability, and Public Service

In politics, honor is essential for maintaining the integrity of democratic processes and fostering public trust in government institutions. Politicians and public officials who act with honor prioritize the needs of their constituents, uphold the principles of transparency and accountability, and are committed to serving the public interest.

Upholding honor in politics involves:

- **Integrity and Ethical Conduct:** Adhering to ethical standards, avoiding conflicts of interest, and making decisions that reflect the best interests of the public.

- **Accountability to Constituents:** Being responsive to the needs and concerns of constituents, and taking responsibility for one's actions and decisions in office.

- **Commitment to Public Service:** Viewing political leadership as a service to the community, rather than a means of personal gain or power.

Honorable politicians, such as Nelson Mandela and Angela Merkel, have demonstrated the value of integrity and ethical leadership in public life. Their commitment to honor has not only shaped their own legacies but has also set a positive example for others in the political arena.

Honor in Community Service: Serving with Integrity and Compassion

Community service is a powerful way to demonstrate honor through acts of kindness, support, and advocacy for others. Whether through volunteering, charitable work, or civic engagement, individuals who serve their communities with honor prioritize the needs of others and act with integrity and compassion.

Upholding honor in community service involves:

- **Respect for All Individuals:** Treating those you serve with dignity, empathy, and understanding, and recognizing the inherent worth of every person.

- **Commitment to Ethical Practices:** Ensuring that service efforts are conducted in an ethical and responsible manner, and that resources are used effectively to benefit the community.

- **Leading by Example:** Demonstrating honorable behavior in all interactions, and inspiring others to engage in service with the same dedication to integrity and respect.

Organizations like Habitat for Humanity, Doctors Without Borders, and local food banks exemplify honor in community service by consistently acting in the best interests of those they serve and maintaining a commitment to ethical standards.

The Role of Individuals in Upholding Honor:

While organizations and institutions play a significant role in promoting honor in professional and public life, individuals also have a crucial part to play. By committing to act with honor in their own roles, whether as employees, leaders, voters, or volunteers, individuals contribute to a broader culture of integrity and accountability.

Practical ways individuals can uphold honor in their professional and public lives include:

- **Modeling Ethical Behavior:** Leading by example and demonstrating honorable actions in all interactions, regardless of the setting.

- **Speaking Up Against Dishonor:** Challenging unethical behavior, advocating for transparency, and holding others accountable when they fall short of honorable standards.

- **Continuous Learning and Reflection:** Engaging in ongoing self-reflection and education on ethical issues, and striving to improve one's understanding and application of honor in all areas of life.

By embracing honor as a guiding principle, individuals can make a meaningful impact on the ethical standards of their workplaces, communities, and society as a whole.

Conclusion

Honor is a vital quality that shapes professional and public life, influencing how individuals conduct themselves in the workplace, business, politics, and community service. It serves as a foundation for trust, credibility, and ethical decision-making, guiding individuals and organizations to act with integrity and accountability.

In leadership, honor sets the standard for behavior, inspiring others to act with integrity and fostering a culture of trust and respect. In decision-making, honor provides a framework for evaluating choices based on ethical considerations and long-term impact. In professional settings, dishonorable behavior can have far-reaching negative consequences, underscoring the importance of upholding honor in all aspects of work and public engagement.

By prioritizing honor in business, politics, and community service, individuals and organizations contribute to a more ethical, just, and trustworthy society. Whether through ethical leadership, corporate responsibility, public service, or community engagement, acting with honor reflects a commitment to the greater good and a dedication to making a positive impact on the world.

As we strive to uphold honor in our professional and public lives, we set a positive example for others and reinforce the values of integrity, accountability, and respect that are essential for the well-being of our communities and society as a whole.

Chapter 8: Honor Across Cultures: A Global Perspective

Honor is a universal concept that transcends borders, yet it manifests differently across cultures. From ancient traditions to modern societies, the perception and practice of honor vary widely, influenced by cultural values, historical contexts, and social norms. Understanding these diverse expressions of honor offers valuable insights into the human experience and helps us appreciate the complexities of ethical behavior in a globalized world. This chapter explores how different cultures perceive and practice honor, identifies common threads and variations, examines how cultural values shape our understanding of honorable behavior, and highlights lessons we can learn from diverse traditions of honor.

Exploring How Different Cultures Perceive and Practice Honor

Honor is a multifaceted concept that is deeply embedded in the cultural fabric of societies around the world. While the essence of honor—adhering to a set of ethical principles and upholding one's values—remains consistent, the way it is expressed and interpreted can vary significantly across cultures.

Honor in Western Cultures: Individualism and Personal Integrity

In many Western cultures, honor is closely associated with individualism and personal integrity. It is often viewed as a personal quality that reflects one's commitment to ethical behavior, honesty, and accountability. The emphasis is on individual actions and the alignment of one's behavior with personal values and principles.

For example, in the United States and Western Europe, honor is frequently linked to the concepts of freedom, self-expression, and personal responsibility. Individuals are encouraged to stand up for their beliefs, act with integrity, and take responsibility for their actions, even when faced with adversity. This individualistic approach to honor places a strong focus on personal ethics and the moral duty to oneself.

In professional settings, honor in Western cultures is often demonstrated through adherence to codes of conduct, transparency, and accountability. Leaders are expected to act with integrity, prioritize ethical decision-making, and uphold the principles of fairness and justice. The emphasis on personal integrity extends to all aspects of life, including family, friendships, and community interactions.

Honor in Eastern Cultures: Collectivism and Social Harmony

In contrast to the individualistic approach of Western cultures, many Eastern cultures emphasize collectivism and social harmony in their understanding of honor. In these societies, honor is often closely tied to the reputation and well-being of the family, community, or group. It reflects a sense of duty to others and the importance of maintaining harmonious relationships.

For example, in Japan, the concept of honor is deeply rooted in the principles of "giri" (duty) and "ninjo" (humanity). Honor is not just a personal attribute but a reflection of one's obligations to family, community, and society. The traditional code of the samurai, known as "bushido," exemplifies the value of honor as a commitment to loyalty, respect, and self-discipline. In contemporary Japanese society, these values continue to influence behavior, with a strong emphasis on humility, respect for others, and the avoidance of actions that might bring shame or dishonor to one's group.

Similarly, in Chinese culture, honor is closely linked to the concept of "mianzi" (face), which represents a person's reputation, dignity, and social standing. Maintaining face is a key aspect of honorable behavior, and individuals are expected to act in ways that preserve their own dignity as well as that of others. This emphasis on social harmony and respect for hierarchy is reflected in everyday interactions, where honor is demonstrated through courteous behavior, deference to authority, and a commitment to fulfilling one's social roles and responsibilities.

Honor in Middle Eastern and Mediterranean Cultures: Family and Community Reputation

In many Middle Eastern and Mediterranean cultures, honor is intricately connected to family and community reputation. It is not solely an individual attribute but a collective value that encompasses the behavior of all family members. Honor is upheld through actions that reflect positively on the family or community, and it is closely guarded against actions that could bring shame or dishonor.

In these cultures, honor often involves strict adherence to social norms, gender roles, and codes of conduct that are designed to protect the family's reputation. For example, in some Middle Eastern societies, the concept of "ird" (family honor) plays a central role in shaping social behavior. Family honor is maintained through the protection of the family's reputation, particularly in matters related to gender, sexuality, and social conduct. Violations of these norms, such as perceived immoral behavior or failure to adhere to cultural expectations, can result in severe social consequences, including ostracism or retribution.

Similarly, in Mediterranean cultures, such as those in Greece and Italy, honor is closely tied to family pride and social standing. The emphasis is on loyalty to family, respect for tradition, and the fulfillment of one's duties to the community. Honor is demonstrated through actions that reflect positively on the family, such as hard work, generosity, and adherence to cultural customs.

Honor in Indigenous Cultures: Respect for Nature and Community

Indigenous cultures around the world often have unique perspectives on honor that are deeply connected to their relationship with nature and the community. Honor is viewed as a holistic concept that encompasses respect for the environment, ancestors, and the interconnectedness of all living beings.

For example, in many Indigenous cultures in North America, honor is closely linked to the principles of respect, reciprocity, and stewardship of the land. Honor is demonstrated through actions that show respect for nature, such as sustainable practices, rituals that honor the earth, and a commitment to preserving cultural traditions. The concept of honor extends beyond individual behavior to include the collective responsibility to care for the community and future generations.

Similarly, in Māori culture in New Zealand, honor is reflected in the concept of "mana," which represents a person's spiritual power, authority, and respect. Mana is not just an individual attribute but is influenced by one's actions, relationships, and connection to the land and ancestors. Upholding mana involves acting with integrity, showing respect for others, and fulfilling one's responsibilities to the community and environment.

These Indigenous perspectives on honor highlight the importance of living in harmony with nature, honoring ancestral wisdom, and recognizing the interconnectedness of all aspects of life.

Common Threads and Variations of Honor Worldwide

While the specific expressions of honor vary across cultures, there are common threads that connect these diverse perspectives. At its core, honor is about upholding values, acting with integrity, and maintaining a sense of dignity and respect. However, the ways in which honor is understood and practiced can differ significantly based on cultural contexts.

Common Threads of Honor

Despite cultural differences, there are several universal themes that are often associated with the concept of honor:

- **Integrity and Ethical Behavior:** Across cultures, honor is linked to the idea of acting in accordance with one's values and ethical principles. Whether in individualistic or collectivist societies, integrity is a key component of honorable behavior.

- **Respect for Others:** Honor involves showing respect for others, whether it is respect for family, community, elders, or authority figures. This respect is often demonstrated through courteous behavior, fulfilling social obligations, and treating others with dignity.

- **Accountability and Responsibility:** Honor includes taking responsibility for one's actions and being accountable to oneself, others, or the community. This sense of accountability is reflected in the willingness to admit mistakes, make amends, and uphold commitments.

- **Protection of Reputation:** In many cultures, honor is closely tied to the protection of one's reputation or the reputation of one's family or group. Maintaining a positive reputation is seen as a reflection of honorable behavior and is often safeguarded through adherence to social norms and ethical conduct.

Variations of Honor Across Cultures

While there are common threads, the specific practices and interpretations of honor can vary widely across cultures. These variations are often influenced by historical, social, and cultural factors:

- **Individualism vs. Collectivism:** In individualistic cultures, honor is often viewed as a personal quality that reflects individual integrity and ethical behavior. In collectivist cultures, honor is more closely tied to the group's reputation, and actions are evaluated based on their impact on the family or community.

- **Gender Roles:** In some cultures, honor is associated with specific gender roles and expectations. For example, in certain Middle Eastern cultures, women's behavior is often closely monitored as a reflection of family honor, while men's honor may be linked to their ability to protect and provide for their families. In contrast, other cultures may have more egalitarian views of honor that apply equally to all genders.

- **Conflict and Resolution:** Different cultures have varying approaches to conflict and how honor is maintained or restored. In some societies, honor may be defended through confrontational means, such as dueling or public challenges. In others, honor is preserved through reconciliation, mediation, and the avoidance of direct confrontation.

- **Religious and Spiritual Influences:** Honor is often shaped by religious and spiritual beliefs, which provide a moral framework for ethical behavior. For example, in many Islamic cultures, honor is closely tied to religious teachings about duty, humility, and the importance of upholding family values. In other cultures, honor may be influenced by spiritual concepts such as karma, ancestral reverence, or the pursuit of spiritual enlightenment.

Understanding these variations allows us to appreciate the diversity of human experience and the ways in which cultural values shape our understanding of honorable behavior.

How Cultural Values Shape Our Understanding of Honorable Behavior

Cultural values play a significant role in shaping how we perceive and practice honor. These values are often transmitted through family, education, religion, and societal norms, influencing our beliefs about what is right, just, and honorable.

The Influence of Family and Community

Family and community are primary sources of cultural values that shape our understanding of honor. From a young age, individuals are taught what behaviors are considered honorable and how to navigate social expectations. Family traditions, stories, and role models all contribute to the development of a sense of honor.

In cultures where family reputation is paramount, individuals may be taught to prioritize actions that reflect positively on the family, such as showing respect for elders, fulfilling familial duties, and adhering to cultural customs. In contrast, in cultures that emphasize personal autonomy, honor may be associated with independent decision-making, personal integrity, and the pursuit of individual goals.

Community values also play a role in defining honor. In collectivist cultures, the emphasis is on contributing to the well-being of the community, maintaining social harmony, and fulfilling one's role within the group. In individualistic cultures, community values may still influence honor, but the focus is often on how individuals can make a positive impact through their personal achievements and ethical conduct.

The Role of Religion and Spirituality

Religion and spirituality are powerful influences on cultural values and perceptions of honor. Many religious traditions provide moral guidelines that define what is considered honorable behavior, such as honesty, humility, compassion, and respect for others.

For example, in Christianity, honor is often associated with living according to the teachings of Jesus, such as loving one's neighbor, forgiving others, and acting with humility and kindness. In Islam, honor is linked to the principles of "iman" (faith), "ihsan" (excellence), and fulfilling one's obligations to God and the community. In Hinduism, honor may be connected to the concept of "dharma," or righteous duty, which involves living in harmony with one's moral responsibilities.

Spiritual beliefs can also shape honor by providing a broader perspective on the interconnectedness of all beings and the importance of ethical behavior in achieving spiritual growth. For example, in Buddhist cultures, honor is associated with the principles of "right action" and "right speech," which are part of the Eightfold Path that guides ethical living.

Social Norms and Expectations

Social norms and expectations are powerful determinants of what is considered honorable behavior in any given culture. These norms dictate how individuals are expected to act in various situations, such as how to show respect, handle conflict, or demonstrate loyalty.

For example, in cultures with a strong emphasis on hierarchy and respect for authority, honor may be demonstrated through deference to elders, adherence to social protocols, and fulfilling one's duties without question. In more egalitarian cultures, honor may be expressed through open communication, collaboration, and the recognition of individual contributions.

Social norms also influence how honor is restored when it is perceived to be compromised. In some cultures, public acts of apology, restitution, or ritual are used to address dishonorable behavior and restore one's standing in the community. In others, private reflection, personal growth, and making amends may be the preferred means of addressing dishonor.

The Impact of Historical and Political Contexts

Historical and political contexts can also shape cultural values and perceptions of honor. Societies that have experienced colonization, conflict, or social upheaval may have distinct understandings of honor that reflect their struggles for identity, autonomy, and justice.

For example, in post-colonial societies, honor may be associated with the preservation of cultural heritage, resistance to oppression, and the assertion of national or ethnic pride. In countries with a history of conflict or civil rights movements, honor may be linked to activism, advocacy for justice, and standing up for marginalized groups.

Political ideologies can also influence honor, particularly in how individuals view their responsibilities to the state, community, or cause. In some contexts, honor may be tied to patriotism, loyalty to a political ideology, or the willingness to make personal sacrifices for the greater good.

Understanding how cultural values shape our perceptions of honor allows us to navigate diverse cultural landscapes with greater empathy, respect, and appreciation for the complexities of human behavior.

Learning from Diverse Traditions of Honor

Exploring diverse traditions of honor offers valuable lessons that can enrich our understanding of ethical behavior and guide us in our own lives. By learning from different cultural perspectives, we can broaden our appreciation of honor and develop a more nuanced approach to ethical living.

Embracing a Holistic View of Honor

One of the key lessons from diverse traditions of honor is the importance of viewing honor as a holistic concept that encompasses not only individual behavior but also relationships, community, and the environment. Indigenous cultures, for example, emphasize the interconnectedness of all living beings and the responsibility to act with honor in a way that respects nature, ancestors, and future generations.

This holistic view of honor encourages us to consider the broader impact of our actions and to strive for a balance between personal integrity and our responsibilities to others. It reminds us that honor is not just about personal achievement but also about contributing to the well-being of our communities and the world around us.

Recognizing the Value of Humility and Respect

Many cultures highlight the importance of humility and respect as central elements of honor. In Eastern and Indigenous traditions, honor is often demonstrated through actions that prioritize the dignity of others, acknowledge one's limitations, and avoid actions that bring unnecessary attention or glory to oneself.

This perspective challenges the notion of honor as solely tied to individual recognition or status and instead emphasizes the value of humility, service, and the quiet fulfillment of one's duties. It encourages us to approach our interactions with others with a sense of respect, empathy, and a recognition of our shared humanity.

Balancing Individual and Collective Honor

Exploring diverse traditions of honor also reveals the balance between individual and collective honor. In collectivist cultures, honor is often seen as a reflection of the group's reputation, while in individualistic cultures, it is viewed as a personal attribute. Both perspectives offer valuable insights into how honor can be practiced in a way that respects both individual autonomy and the importance of community.

Learning from these traditions can help us navigate the tension between personal integrity and our responsibilities to others, allowing us to honor our own values while also contributing to the greater good. It reminds us that honor is not an isolated concept but one that is deeply connected to our relationships and our roles within society.

Adapting Honor to Contemporary Challenges

Finally, diverse traditions of honor provide valuable lessons on how to adapt the concept of honor to contemporary challenges. As societies evolve and face new ethical dilemmas, the principles of honor can serve as a guiding framework for navigating complex issues such as digital ethics, environmental sustainability, social justice, and global citizenship.

By drawing on the rich tapestry of cultural perspectives on honor, we can develop a more adaptable and inclusive approach to ethical living that addresses the needs of our interconnected world. This adaptability allows us to honor both our cultural heritage and our shared responsibility to create a just and equitable future for all.

Conclusion

Honor is a universal concept that transcends cultural boundaries, yet its expressions and interpretations are shaped by the unique values, histories, and social norms of each society. By exploring how different cultures perceive and practice honor, we gain a deeper appreciation for the diversity of human experience and the common threads that connect us all.

Honor serves as a guiding principle that influences our actions, shapes our relationships, and reflects our commitment to ethical behavior. Whether through individual integrity, respect for community, or a holistic view of our responsibilities to the world, honor provides a powerful framework for living a meaningful and principled life.

Learning from diverse traditions of honor enriches our understanding of what it means to act honorably and challenges us to consider the broader impact of our actions. It encourages us to embrace a more inclusive and adaptable approach to honor, one that respects both individual and collective values and addresses the ethical challenges of our globalized world.

As we strive to uphold honor in our own lives, we can draw inspiration from the rich cultural tapestry of human experience, recognizing that honor is not a static or one-dimensional concept but a dynamic and evolving expression of our shared humanity. By embracing the lessons of honor from around the world, we contribute to a more compassionate, just, and interconnected world where the principles of integrity, respect, and responsibility are valued and upheld.

Chapter 9: Challenges to Honor: Temptations and Tests

Honor is a guiding principle that helps individuals navigate life with integrity and dignity. However, the path to maintaining honor is often fraught with challenges, including temptations, fears, and external pressures. These challenges test our commitment to our values and can sometimes lead us astray. Understanding these obstacles, and developing strategies to overcome them, is crucial for staying true to one's values in difficult situations. This chapter explores common challenges to maintaining honor, such as greed, fear, and peer pressure, provides strategies for upholding one's values, discusses how to recover from moments of dishonor, and highlights the importance of resilience in upholding honor.

Identifying Common Challenges to Maintaining Honor

Maintaining honor is a continuous effort that requires vigilance and self-awareness. Life presents numerous challenges that can test our resolve and tempt us to compromise our values. Recognizing these challenges is the first step in preparing to meet them with integrity.

Greed: The Temptation of Self-Interest

Greed, or the excessive desire for wealth, power, or status, is a powerful temptation that can lead individuals to act dishonorably. It often drives people to prioritize their own self-interest over ethical considerations, leading to actions such as dishonesty, exploitation, or corruption. Greed can manifest in various forms, from the pursuit of financial gain at the expense of others to the desire for recognition that overrides the importance of fairness and integrity.

For example, in the business world, greed may tempt individuals to cut corners, engage in fraudulent activities, or exploit others to maximize profits. In politics, it can lead to corruption, abuse of power, and decisions that benefit a select few rather than the broader community. Greed undermines honor by prioritizing personal gain over ethical principles, damaging relationships, reputations, and trust.

Fear: The Barrier to Courage and Integrity

Fear is another significant challenge to maintaining honor. It can paralyze individuals, preventing them from acting in accordance with their values, especially when doing so involves personal risk or potential loss. Fear of failure, rejection, punishment, or harm can lead individuals to compromise their integrity or remain silent in the face of wrongdoing.

For example, a whistleblower who fears retaliation may choose to stay silent rather than expose unethical practices within their organization. Similarly, an individual who fears social ostracism may conform to peer pressure rather than standing up for what they know is right. Fear often presents a stark test of honor, challenging individuals to summon the courage to act ethically despite the potential consequences.

Peer Pressure: The Influence of Social Conformity

Peer pressure, or the influence of others to conform to certain behaviors or attitudes, is a pervasive challenge that can undermine honor. The desire to fit in, gain approval, or avoid conflict can lead individuals to act in ways that contradict their values. Peer pressure can be particularly strong in group settings, where the fear of standing out or being judged can outweigh the commitment to ethical behavior.

For example, a student who values honesty may feel pressured to cheat on an exam because their peers are doing so. In the workplace, employees may feel compelled to participate in unethical practices if they perceive that doing so is the norm or expected by their colleagues or superiors. Peer pressure can erode honor by encouraging individuals to prioritize social acceptance over personal integrity.

Rationalization: The Justification of Dishonorable Behavior

Rationalization is the process of justifying unethical behavior by creating excuses or minimizing the perceived impact of one's actions. It is a cognitive defense mechanism that allows individuals to engage in dishonorable behavior while maintaining a sense of self-righteousness or moral superiority. Rationalization can take many forms, such as downplaying the significance of a lie, blaming circumstances for unethical actions, or convincing oneself that "everyone else is doing it."

For example, an employee who falsifies financial records might rationalize their behavior by believing that it is necessary for the company's survival or that "it's just a one-time thing." This mindset allows individuals to sidestep their ethical responsibilities and act dishonorably without fully confronting the implications of their actions.

Complacency: The Erosion of Ethical Vigilance

Complacency, or a lack of vigilance in upholding ethical standards, can gradually erode honor over time. When individuals become complacent, they may overlook small ethical lapses, fail to challenge unethical behavior, or neglect the importance of consistently acting with integrity. This erosion of honor often occurs incrementally, as small compromises accumulate and lead to larger ethical failures.

For example, a professional who initially overlooks minor ethical violations may eventually become desensitized to more significant breaches of conduct. Complacency can result in a gradual departure from one's values, making it increasingly difficult to maintain honor in the face of challenges.

Strategies for Staying True to One's Values in Difficult Situations

Maintaining honor in the face of challenges requires deliberate effort and a proactive approach to ethical decision-making. By developing strategies to uphold one's values, individuals can navigate difficult situations with integrity and resilience.

Clarify Your Core Values and Commit to Them

One of the most effective ways to maintain honor is to have a clear understanding of your core values and to make a conscious commitment to uphold them. Reflecting on what matters most to you—such as honesty, fairness, compassion, or accountability—provides a solid foundation for ethical behavior. When faced with difficult decisions, refer back to these core values as a guide.

Creating a personal code of ethics or a set of guiding principles can help reinforce your commitment to honor. By articulating your values and intentions, you establish a clear standard for your behavior and decision-making, making it easier to stay true to your principles when tested.

Practice Ethical Decision-Making: A Framework for Honor

Developing a structured approach to ethical decision-making can help you navigate challenging situations with honor. A common framework for ethical decision-making includes the following steps:

- **Identify the Ethical Dilemma:** Clearly define the situation and the ethical issues involved. Acknowledge the potential conflicts between your values and external pressures.

- **Evaluate the Consequences:** Consider the potential outcomes of each course of action, including the impact on yourself, others, and the broader community. Weigh the short-term and long-term consequences of your decisions.

- **Consult Your Values:** Reflect on how each option aligns with your core values and ethical principles. Prioritize actions that uphold your honor, even if they involve personal sacrifice or discomfort.

- **Seek Guidance:** When faced with complex or uncertain situations, seek guidance from trusted mentors, colleagues, or ethical resources. Discussing your dilemma with others can provide valuable perspectives and reinforce your commitment to honor.

- **Make a Decision and Act with Integrity:** Once you have evaluated your options, make a decision that reflects your values and act with integrity. Be willing to take responsibility for your actions and their consequences.

Cultivate Moral Courage: Facing Fear with Honor

Moral courage is the ability to act in accordance with your values, even when faced with fear, uncertainty, or potential loss. Cultivating moral courage involves recognizing fear as a natural response but choosing to act with integrity despite it. To build moral courage:

- **Start with Small Acts of Courage:** Practice standing up for your values in everyday situations, such as speaking up in a meeting or addressing a minor ethical concern. These small acts of courage build confidence and prepare you for more significant challenges.

- **Focus on the Bigger Picture:** Remind yourself of the broader impact of your actions, such as the positive influence you can have on others or the importance of setting a good example. This perspective can help you overcome fear by connecting your actions to a greater purpose.

- **Embrace Vulnerability:** Acknowledge that acting honorably may involve taking risks, making mistakes, or facing criticism. Embrace vulnerability as part of the process of living with integrity, and be willing to learn from setbacks.

Build a Supportive Network: Allies in Honor

Surrounding yourself with individuals who share your commitment to honor can provide valuable support and reinforcement in challenging times. A supportive network of friends, colleagues, mentors, and family members can offer encouragement, advice, and a sense of accountability.

Seek out relationships with people who inspire you to uphold your values and who challenge you to act with integrity. Engage in open conversations about ethical dilemmas, share your experiences, and learn from the perspectives of others. A strong support network can help you stay grounded and resilient in the face of temptations and tests.

Develop Resilience: Bouncing Back from Dishonor

Resilience is the ability to recover from setbacks, adapt to challenges, and continue moving forward with integrity. In the context of honor, resilience involves learning from moments of dishonor and using those experiences to strengthen your commitment to ethical behavior.

To develop resilience:

- **Reflect on Mistakes:** When you fall short of your values, take time to reflect on what went wrong, why it happened, and what you can learn from the experience. Avoid self-condemnation, and instead focus on growth and improvement.

- **Make Amends:** If your actions have harmed others, take responsibility and make amends. Apologize sincerely, seek forgiveness, and take steps to repair the damage. Demonstrating accountability and a willingness to correct your mistakes is a key aspect of resilience and honor.

- **Reaffirm Your Commitment:** Use moments of dishonor as an opportunity to reaffirm your commitment to your values. Reflect on the importance of honor in your life and renew your dedication to acting with integrity, even when it is difficult.

How to Recover and Learn from Moments of Dishonor

No one is immune to making mistakes or falling short of their values. Moments of dishonor are part of the human experience, but they do not have to define us. By approaching these moments with humility, accountability, and a willingness to learn, we can recover and continue to uphold honor.

Acknowledge the Dishonor: Facing the Truth

The first step in recovering from a moment of dishonor is to acknowledge it honestly and without excuses. This requires facing the truth of what happened, accepting responsibility for your actions, and recognizing the impact they had on others. Acknowledgment is not about self-punishment; it is about taking ownership of your behavior and being honest with yourself and those affected.

Seek Forgiveness and Make Amends

Seeking forgiveness is an important part of the recovery process, both for repairing relationships and for restoring your own sense of integrity. A sincere apology involves acknowledging the harm caused, expressing genuine remorse, and committing to change. Making amends may also involve taking concrete steps to address the consequences of your actions, such as offering restitution, correcting the error, or making changes to prevent a recurrence.

Reflect and Learn: Turning Dishonor into Growth

Reflection is a powerful tool for learning from moments of dishonor. Take time to reflect on what led to the dishonorable behavior, such as underlying fears, pressures, or rationalizations. Consider what you could have done differently and how you can apply those lessons to future situations.

Reflection also involves examining your values and reaffirming your commitment to them. Use the experience as an opportunity to deepen your understanding of honor and to strengthen your resolve to act with integrity in the future.

Forgive Yourself: Moving Forward with Compassion

Forgiving yourself is an essential part of recovering from dishonor. Self-forgiveness involves letting go of self-blame and recognizing that everyone makes mistakes. It is about treating yourself with the same compassion and understanding that you would offer to others in similar situations.

Self-forgiveness does not mean ignoring the impact of your actions or avoiding responsibility; rather, it is about acknowledging your imperfections and choosing to move forward with a renewed commitment to honor. By forgiving yourself, you free yourself from the burden of past mistakes and open the door to personal growth and resilience.

Recommit to Honor: A Path of Continuous Improvement

Recovery from dishonor is not a one-time event but an ongoing process of recommitting to your values and striving for continuous improvement. Recommitment involves setting new goals, developing strategies to uphold honor, and remaining vigilant against the challenges that may arise.

Recognize that honor is a journey, not a destination, and that each day presents opportunities to act with integrity, courage, and respect. By embracing this journey, you can transform moments of dishonor into catalysts for personal growth and a deeper understanding of what it means to live honorably.

The Importance of Resilience in Upholding Honor

Resilience is a key quality that supports the maintenance of honor over time. It enables individuals to persevere through challenges, recover from setbacks, and remain steadfast in their commitment to ethical behavior. Resilience is not about never failing; it is about how you respond when faced with tests of your values.

Building Emotional Resilience: Managing Stress and Pressure

Emotional resilience involves the ability to manage stress, cope with adversity, and maintain a positive outlook even in difficult circumstances. Building emotional resilience can help you navigate the pressures and temptations that challenge honor. Techniques for building emotional resilience include:

- **Mindfulness and Self-Awareness:** Practicing mindfulness helps you stay present and attuned to your emotions, making it easier to recognize when fear, anger, or other emotions are influencing your behavior.

- **Healthy Coping Strategies:** Developing healthy ways to cope with stress, such as exercise, journaling, meditation, or talking to a trusted friend, can help you manage difficult emotions and reduce the likelihood of acting dishonorably under pressure.

- **Positive Self-Talk:** Replacing negative or self-defeating thoughts with positive affirmations and constructive self-talk can boost your confidence and reinforce your commitment to honor.

Developing Moral Resilience: Staying True to Your Values

Moral resilience is the ability to stay true to your values, even when faced with ethical challenges or external pressures. It involves cultivating a strong sense of purpose and a commitment to acting with integrity, regardless of the circumstances.

To develop moral resilience:

- **Regularly Revisit Your Values:** Keep your values at the forefront of your mind by regularly reflecting on them and considering how they apply to your daily decisions and actions.

- **Anticipate Challenges:** Think ahead about potential situations where your honor might be tested, and plan how you will respond. Preparing for challenges in advance can help you stay grounded and make decisions that align with your values.

- **Commit to Lifelong Learning:** Continuously seek opportunities to learn about ethics, honor, and personal development. Engage in discussions, read books, attend workshops, or seek mentorship to deepen your understanding and strengthen your resilience.

Embracing a Growth Mindset: Learning from Challenges

A growth mindset is the belief that abilities and qualities can be developed through effort, learning, and perseverance.

Embracing a growth mindset allows you to view challenges to honor as opportunities for learning and growth, rather than as insurmountable obstacles.

When faced with setbacks, approach them with curiosity and a willingness to learn. Ask yourself what you can take away from the experience and how you can apply those lessons to future situations. A growth mindset encourages resilience by helping you see challenges as part of the journey of upholding honor.

Fostering Community Resilience: Supporting Each Other in Honor

Resilience is not just an individual quality; it is also a collective one. Fostering community resilience involves creating environments where individuals feel supported, valued, and empowered to act honorably. This can be achieved through:

- **Creating Safe Spaces:** Establish safe and supportive spaces where individuals can discuss ethical dilemmas, share their experiences, and seek guidance without fear of judgment.

- **Encouraging Collective Accountability:** Promote a culture of accountability where everyone is responsible for upholding honor and supporting each other in ethical decision-making.

- **Celebrating Acts of Honor:** Recognize and celebrate acts of honor, both big and small, to reinforce the importance of integrity and inspire others to follow suit.

By fostering a sense of community resilience, you create a network of support that strengthens everyone's ability to uphold honor in the face of challenges.

Conclusion

Honor is a guiding principle that helps individuals navigate life with integrity and dignity, but it is not without its challenges. Temptations such as greed, fear, and peer pressure can test our commitment to our values and lead us astray. However, by developing strategies to uphold honor, cultivating resilience, and learning from moments of dishonor, we can navigate these challenges and continue to live with integrity.

Resilience is a key quality in the pursuit of honor, enabling us to recover from setbacks, adapt to challenges, and remain steadfast in our commitment to ethical behavior. By embracing resilience, we can transform challenges into opportunities for growth, deepen our understanding of honor, and inspire others to act with integrity.

Ultimately, honor is not about perfection but about the ongoing journey of striving to live in accordance with our values, even when faced with difficult tests. By remaining vigilant, seeking support, and continuously recommitting to our principles, we can uphold honor and make a positive impact on the world around us.

Chapter 10: Living with Honor: Daily Practice and Personal Growth

Honor is not a static trait or a one-time achievement; it is a dynamic and ongoing commitment that permeates every aspect of life. Living with honor requires integrating ethical principles into everyday actions, consistently striving to uphold one's values, and continuously growing as an individual. This chapter explores how to integrate honor into daily life and decision-making, emphasizes the continuous journey of striving for honorable behavior, provides guidance on inspiring honorable actions in others, and discusses the legacy of honor—how principled living can leave a lasting impact on those around us and future generations.

Integrating Honor into Everyday Life and Decision-Making

Living with honor means making a conscious effort to align one's actions, decisions, and interactions with core values and ethical principles. It involves cultivating habits that reflect integrity, accountability, and respect, both in small everyday choices and in more significant life decisions.

Start with Self-Reflection: Knowing Your Values and Principles

The foundation of living with honor is a clear understanding of your personal values and ethical principles. Take time for self-reflection to identify what matters most to you—whether it is honesty, kindness, responsibility, courage, or any other virtue. Reflecting on these values allows you to set a standard for your behavior and serves as a compass for decision-making.

To start, consider the following steps:

- **Identify Your Core Values:** Write down the values that you hold most dear. These might include integrity, compassion, fairness, humility, or loyalty. Consider how these values align with your actions and decisions.

- **Define Your Principles:** Beyond identifying values, articulate specific principles that guide your behavior. For example, if one of your core values is honesty, a guiding principle might be, "I will always speak the truth, even when it is difficult."

- **Reflect Regularly:** Make self-reflection a regular practice. This might involve journaling, meditation, or simply taking a few moments each day to consider whether your actions align with your values. Regular reflection helps keep you accountable and aware of areas for growth.

Apply Ethical Principles to Daily Decisions

Living with honor involves applying ethical principles to everyday decisions, no matter how small. Every action, from how you treat a colleague to how you handle personal challenges, offers an opportunity to demonstrate honor. By approaching daily decisions with a mindset of integrity, you cultivate a habit of ethical behavior that extends to all aspects of life.

Here are some ways to apply honor in daily decisions:

- **Prioritize Honesty:** Commit to being truthful in your interactions, whether with friends, family, or strangers. Honesty fosters trust and reflects a commitment to integrity, even in situations where it may be tempting to bend the truth.

- **Choose Kindness:** Make kindness a daily practice. Simple acts of kindness, such as offering a smile, helping someone in need, or showing appreciation, reflect honorable behavior and positively impact those around you.

- **Embrace Responsibility:** Take responsibility for your actions, including mistakes. Owning up to errors, apologizing when necessary, and making amends are critical aspects of living with honor.

- **Show Respect:** Treat everyone you encounter with respect, regardless of their background, status, or beliefs. Respectful interactions demonstrate a recognition of others' dignity and value.

Make Decisions with Integrity: A Framework for Honorable Living

Integrating honor into decision-making involves a conscious effort to evaluate choices through the lens of your values. Use the following framework to guide your decisions:

- **Assess the Situation:** Clearly define the decision or challenge at hand. Consider the context, the stakeholders involved, and any ethical dilemmas that may arise.

- **Reflect on Your Values:** Ask yourself how each potential action aligns with your core values and principles. Will this decision uphold your commitment to honor, or will it compromise your integrity?

- **Evaluate the Impact:** Consider the potential consequences of your decision on yourself and others. Aim to choose actions that promote positive outcomes, fairness, and respect.

- **Seek Guidance:** When faced with particularly complex or challenging decisions, seek advice from trusted mentors, colleagues, or loved ones who share your commitment to honor. Their perspectives can offer valuable insights and help you navigate difficult situations.

- **Commit to Action:** Once you have evaluated your options, make a decision that aligns with your values, and commit to following through with integrity. Be prepared to stand by your decision, even if it involves personal sacrifice.

Practice Accountability: Holding Yourself to a Higher Standard

Accountability is a crucial component of living with honor. It involves holding yourself to a high standard of behavior, taking responsibility for your actions, and being willing to correct course when necessary. Practicing accountability means recognizing that you are not infallible and that there will be times when you fall short of your ideals.

To practice accountability:

- **Set Personal Benchmarks:** Establish clear benchmarks for what honorable behavior looks like in your daily life. This could include setting goals for how you handle conflicts, interact with others, or make decisions.

- **Monitor Your Actions:** Regularly review your behavior to ensure it aligns with your values. If you notice areas where you have fallen short, take immediate steps to address and rectify the situation.

- **Be Transparent:** Be open about your mistakes and shortcomings. Honesty about your imperfections demonstrates humility and reinforces your commitment to honor.

By integrating these practices into your daily life, you create a foundation of honor that guides your actions, decisions, and interactions with others.

The Continuous Journey of Striving for Honorable Behavior

Living with honor is not a destination but a continuous journey. It involves ongoing self-improvement, learning from experiences, and striving to uphold one's values in all circumstances. This journey is marked by both successes and challenges, but each step offers an opportunity for growth and reflection.

Embrace the Process of Growth: Learning from Challenges

The path to honorable living is rarely straightforward. It is a process that involves navigating challenges, making mistakes, and learning from each experience. Rather than striving for perfection, focus on the commitment to continuous growth and improvement.

- **Learn from Mistakes:** View mistakes as valuable learning opportunities. When you fall short of your ideals, take time to reflect on what went wrong and what you can do differently in the future. This mindset of growth fosters resilience and reinforces your commitment to honor.

- **Adapt to Changing Circumstances:** Life is dynamic, and circumstances change. Honor involves adapting to new challenges and remaining true to your values, even when the path forward is unclear. Flexibility and openness to change are essential for maintaining integrity in a complex world.

- **Celebrate Progress:** Acknowledge and celebrate your progress along the journey. Recognizing the small victories, such as choosing kindness in a difficult moment or making a challenging but ethical decision, reinforces your commitment to honorable behavior.

Set Intentions for Honor: Daily Practices for Ethical Living

Setting daily intentions can help you stay focused on living with honor. Intentions are commitments you make to yourself about how you want to show up in the world. By setting specific intentions each day, you remind yourself of your commitment to integrity and create a framework for honorable behavior.

Consider setting daily intentions such as:

- "Today, I will act with kindness and patience in all my interactions."

- "I will prioritize honesty, even when it is difficult or uncomfortable."

- "I will listen to others with an open heart and mind, showing respect for their perspectives."

These intentions serve as reminders of your values and guide your actions throughout the day. By making intentions a regular part of your routine, you reinforce your commitment to honor and create a habit of ethical living.

Engage in Regular Reflection: A Practice of Self-Awareness

Regular reflection is an essential part of the journey toward honorable behavior. Reflection allows you to assess your actions, consider how they align with your values, and identify areas for growth. It also provides an opportunity to celebrate your successes and recommit to your principles.

Consider incorporating reflection into your routine in the following ways:

- **Journaling:** Write about your experiences, decisions, and interactions. Reflect on what went well, where you faced challenges, and how you can continue to grow in your commitment to honor.

- **Mindfulness Practices:** Engage in mindfulness or meditation practices that encourage self-awareness and introspection. Mindfulness helps you stay present and attuned to your thoughts, feelings, and actions.

- **Regular Check-Ins:** Set aside time each week or month to review your progress. Ask yourself questions such as, "How have I lived up to my values this week?" and "What can I do to improve my commitment to honor?"

By making reflection a regular practice, you stay connected to your values and maintain a sense of accountability to yourself.

Cultivate Humility: Embracing Imperfection and Openness to Growth

Humility is a cornerstone of honorable behavior. It involves recognizing that you are not perfect and that there is always room for growth and improvement. Cultivating humility allows you to approach your journey with an open mind, a willingness to learn, and a commitment to continuous self-improvement.

- **Acknowledge Your Limitations:** Accept that you will make mistakes and that you do not have all the answers. This acknowledgment fosters a growth mindset and encourages you to seek out opportunities for learning and development.

- **Be Open to Feedback:** Embrace feedback from others, whether it is positive or constructive. Feedback provides valuable insights into how your actions impact others and offers guidance for how to align more closely with your values.

- **Practice Gratitude:** Cultivate a sense of gratitude for the lessons and experiences that shape your journey. Gratitude fosters resilience and helps you stay focused on the positive aspects of your growth.

Humility is not about diminishing your self-worth; it is about recognizing the value of ongoing growth and remaining open to the lessons that life offers.

How to Inspire and Encourage Honorable Actions in Others

Living with honor not only impacts your own life but also has the power to inspire and influence those around you. By modeling honorable behavior, encouraging others, and fostering a culture of integrity, you can create a positive ripple effect that extends beyond yourself.

Lead by Example: Be a Role Model of Honor

One of the most effective ways to inspire honorable actions in others is to lead by example. Your actions, decisions, and interactions set the tone for those around you, whether in your personal relationships, workplace, or community. By consistently demonstrating integrity, respect, and accountability, you encourage others to do the same.

- **Be Consistent:** Strive to align your actions with your values consistently, even in challenging situations. Consistency builds trust and credibility, showing others that you are committed to honor.

- **Demonstrate Integrity:** Act with integrity in all aspects of your life, from keeping your promises to being honest about your limitations. Integrity inspires confidence and respect, encouraging others to value ethical behavior.

- **Practice Empathy:** Show empathy and understanding in your interactions. By treating others with kindness and respect, you create an environment where honorable behavior is valued and encouraged.

Encourage Open Dialogue: Creating Space for Ethical Conversations

Encouraging open dialogue about ethics, values, and honorable behavior can foster a culture of integrity and accountability. Create opportunities for conversations about what it means to live with honor, and invite others to share their perspectives and experiences.

- **Host Discussions:** Organize discussions, workshops, or team meetings focused on ethical decision-making and the importance of honor. These conversations provide a platform for exploring values and sharing insights.

- **Ask Thought-Provoking Questions:** Encourage others to reflect on their values and actions by asking thought-provoking questions. For example, "What does honor mean to you?" or "How do you navigate ethical challenges in your life?"

- **Create Safe Spaces:** Foster a safe and supportive environment where individuals feel comfortable sharing their thoughts and concerns. A culture of open dialogue promotes transparency and mutual respect.

Recognize and Celebrate Honorable Actions: Reinforcing Positive Behavior

Recognizing and celebrating honorable actions reinforces the value of integrity and encourages others to continue acting with honor. Positive reinforcement can take many forms, from verbal acknowledgment to formal recognition.

- **Offer Praise and Acknowledgment:** When you see someone acting honorably, take the time to acknowledge their actions. A simple "Thank you for your honesty" or "I admire your commitment to fairness" can have a significant impact.

- **Highlight Role Models:** Share stories of individuals who exemplify honorable behavior, whether within your community or on a broader scale. Highlighting role models provides inspiration and reinforces the importance of honor.

- **Create Recognition Programs:** In professional or organizational settings, consider implementing recognition programs that reward ethical behavior and integrity. Formal recognition can motivate others to prioritize honorable actions.

Provide Guidance and Support: Mentoring for Honor

Mentoring others in the practice of honor is a powerful way to foster ethical behavior and personal growth. As a mentor, you have the opportunity to guide, support, and encourage individuals on their journey toward living with honor.

- **Offer Guidance:** Share your experiences, insights, and lessons learned with those you mentor. Provide guidance on navigating ethical challenges and making decisions that align with core values.

- **Be a Source of Encouragement:** Offer encouragement and support, especially when individuals face difficult situations. Your encouragement can bolster their confidence and reinforce their commitment to honor.

- **Foster Accountability:** Help those you mentor stay accountable to their values by regularly checking in on their progress and offering constructive feedback.

Mentorship is not about imposing your values on others but about helping them discover and embrace their own commitment to honor.

The Legacy of Honor: Leaving a Lasting Impact Through Principled Living

Living with honor extends beyond the present moment; it is about creating a lasting impact that resonates with others and contributes to a better world. The legacy of honor is not measured by accolades or achievements but by the positive influence you have on the lives of others and the example you set for future generations.

Creating a Positive Ripple Effect: The Impact of Honorable Actions

Every act of honor, no matter how small, has the potential to create a positive ripple effect. Your actions inspire others to act with integrity, and their actions, in turn, inspire others. This chain reaction of honorable behavior can lead to meaningful change in families, communities, workplaces, and society at large.

- **Influencing Future Generations:** By modeling honorable behavior, you set an example for future generations. Children, students, and young professionals learn from observing how you navigate challenges and uphold your values. Your commitment to honor becomes a guiding light for those who follow in your footsteps.

- **Contributing to a Culture of Integrity:** Your actions contribute to the broader cultural landscape, shaping the values and norms of your community or organization. By prioritizing honor, you help create a culture where ethical behavior is valued, expected, and celebrated.

- **Leaving a Legacy of Trust and Respect:** A legacy of honor is characterized by trust, respect, and positive relationships. When others remember you for your integrity, kindness, and commitment to your values, you leave behind a legacy that transcends time.

Building Lasting Relationships: The Role of Honor in Connection

Honor plays a crucial role in building and sustaining meaningful relationships. By acting with integrity and respect, you cultivate trust, deepen connections, and create bonds that stand the test of time.

- **Strengthening Trust:** Trust is the foundation of all relationships, and honor is essential for building and maintaining that trust. When others know they can rely on you to act with integrity, they feel secure in their connection with you.

- **Fostering Mutual Respect:** Honorable behavior fosters mutual respect, where both parties value and appreciate each other's contributions. This respect creates a sense of equality and partnership that enhances the quality of the relationship.

- **Nurturing Empathy and Understanding:** Living with honor involves showing empathy and understanding toward others. This approach fosters open communication, reduces conflict, and strengthens the emotional bonds that connect us.

Creating Ethical Leadership: Guiding with Honor

Leadership is a powerful platform for demonstrating honor and influencing others. Ethical leaders prioritize integrity, transparency, and accountability, setting a standard for others to follow. Whether in a professional, community, or personal context, ethical leadership can leave a lasting legacy of honor.

- **Inspire Ethical Behavior:** As a leader, your actions serve as a model for those you lead. By prioritizing honor in your decision-making, communication, and interactions, you inspire others to act with integrity and contribute to a culture of ethical behavior.

- **Empower Others:** Ethical leaders empower others by fostering a sense of agency, accountability, and responsibility. They encourage individuals to embrace their own values and make decisions that align with their principles.

- **Lead with Purpose:** Honorable leaders are driven by a sense of purpose and a commitment to making a positive impact. They prioritize the well-being of others, advocate for justice and fairness, and strive to create a legacy that reflects their core values.

Contributing to Positive Change: Honor as a Force for Good

Living with honor positions you as a force for positive change in the world. Whether through acts of service, advocacy, or simply leading by example, your commitment to honor contributes to a more just, compassionate, and ethical society.

- **Advocate for Justice and Fairness:** Use your voice to advocate for causes that align with your values. Whether it is supporting social justice, environmental sustainability, or community development, your actions can help drive meaningful change.

- **Engage in Service:** Honor involves giving back to others and contributing to the greater good. Engage in acts of service, volunteer work, or charitable efforts that reflect your commitment to making a positive impact.

- **Promote Inclusivity and Respect:** Champion inclusivity, respect, and equality in all aspects of life. By advocating for the rights and dignity of others, you help create a world where everyone is valued and honored.

Conclusion

Living with honor is a continuous journey of striving for ethical behavior, integrating values into everyday life, and inspiring others to act with integrity. It is a commitment to personal growth, accountability, and the pursuit of a principled life. By embracing honor as a daily practice, you create a foundation of integrity that guides your actions, shapes your relationships, and influences those around you.

The legacy of honor is not defined by grand gestures or accolades but by the positive impact you have on others and the example you set through principled living. Whether through small acts of kindness, ethical decision-making, or leadership with integrity, your commitment to honor leaves a lasting mark on the world.

As you navigate the complexities of life, remember that honor is not about perfection but about the ongoing effort to align your actions with your values. By continuously striving for honorable behavior, embracing the lessons of each experience, and encouraging others to do the same, you contribute to a more ethical, compassionate, and connected world. The legacy of honor is one of trust, respect, and positive change—an enduring testament to the power of principled living.

Conclusion: Embracing Honor as a Way of Life

Honor is more than a lofty ideal or a distant virtue; it is a foundational concept that permeates every aspect of our lives. It begins with a commitment to integrity and truthfulness, the core pillars that guide our actions and decisions. By embracing these principles, we align ourselves with a path of honesty, transparency, and accountability. Honor is not just about what we do when others are watching; it is a moral obligation that compels us to act with integrity, even in the most private moments.

Throughout this book, we have explored how honor manifests in various dimensions of life, from standing up for justice and fairness to cultivating honorable behavior in our personal and professional relationships. In every context, honor serves as a compass, directing us toward ethical decisions and actions that reflect our highest values. Whether advocating for the rights of others, making principled choices at work, or nurturing trust in our personal connections, honor is the thread that weaves integrity, respect, and compassion into the fabric of our daily lives.

The journey of honor is not without its challenges. We are constantly tested by temptations, fears, and external pressures that can lead us astray. Greed, peer pressure, and the desire for acceptance are powerful forces that can compromise our commitment to honor. Yet, it is precisely in these moments of challenge that the true strength of honor is revealed. By developing resilience and moral courage—the backbone of honor—we can navigate these tests and remain steadfast in our values. Learning to recognize and confront these challenges equips us to make decisions that uphold our integrity, even when the easier path may be to compromise.

Honor is not confined to a single culture or tradition; it is a universal value that transcends borders. From East to West, from ancient traditions to modern societies, honor is expressed in diverse ways, reflecting the rich tapestry of human experience. By exploring these cultural perspectives, we gain a deeper appreciation for the common threads that unite us, as well as the unique variations that enrich our understanding of honorable behavior. This global perspective encourages us to approach honor with empathy, respect, and an openness to learning from one another.

Ultimately, living with honor is a continuous journey of personal growth and self-improvement. It is about integrating ethical principles into our daily lives and making a conscious effort to align our actions with our values. It involves regular self-reflection, setting intentions, and striving to be better each day. Living with honor is not about achieving perfection; it is about the ongoing commitment to be true to ourselves and to act in ways that contribute to the greater good.

As we conclude this exploration of honor, let us remember that honor is not a destination but a way of life. It is the legacy we leave behind through our actions, our choices, and the impact we have on others. By embracing honor as a guiding principle, we can inspire those around us, foster a more just and compassionate world, and live a life that is truly worth honoring.

About the Author

Tom is a Personal Safety Consultant who has taught in 25 countries, the founder of Invincible: Performance Optimization Coaching, a Motivational Profiling Analyst, an engaging speaker, an avid traveler who has visited 40 countries, and an author of fiction and non-fiction books.

Tom has an interesting background teaching the use of weapons to foreign and domestic government agencies. He is also a Motivational Profiler, a high-performance coach, and author. To learn more about Tom, he invites readers to visit his website.

www.tomsotis.com
tom@tomsotis.com

Other books by Tom Sotis

The Protégé

Asymmetrical Warfare

The Way of Tactics

Sharp Strategies

The Science of Motivation

Scientific Athletic Motivation

Unmasking Predators

Badass Warriors of Personal Combat

Assassination in America

Against Overwhelming Odds

Global Crime Syndicates

Bounty Hunters

Global Knife Culture

Alexander the Great

Assassins for Freedom

Truly Safer

The Character Code

The Art of Character

Timeless Wisdom

Votes, Guns, and Grit

The Rattan Curtain